Dating Old Photographs

Robert Pols

FEDERATION OF FAMILY HISTORY SOCIETIES

Published by
The Federation of Family History Societies (Publications) Ltd
The Benson Room,
Birmingham and Midland Institute,
Margaret Street, Birmingham B3 3BS

First published 1992
Reprinted 1993
Second edition 1995

ISBN 1-86006-013-7

Printed by Oxuniprint, Walton Street, Oxford OX2 6DP

Contents

Introduction

"The fact is, our governor's a friend of the people, and don't mind losing a little money. He's determined that everybody shall have a portrait, from the highest to the lowest. Indeed, next Sunday he do talk of taking them for threepence-ha'penny, and if that ain't philandery, what is?"

Thus, Mayhew records, a Victorian street-photographer's assistant explained his employer's policy. The fact that this explanation was being used to justify a price rise from sixpence to eightpence (if that ain't logic, what is?) may perhaps be overlooked. What matters is the ubiquity of the photographer and the increasing cheapness of the photograph in Victorian England. At the beginning of Victoria's reign the invention of photography was announced; by the end of her reign the day of the snapshot had dawned.

Photography was and is a staggering invention. It brought our ancestors face to face with themselves, and it brings us face to face with them. Not surprisingly, therefore, photographs, whether a full set of albums or a battered handful of pictures, form an important and treasured part of many a family archive. They provide a window through which we gain a glimpse of our own past. But the view through the window is not always clear, and the aim of this small book is, in effect, to dust its glass. More precisely, the intention is to help with understanding the photos which have been handed down, with identifying them, and with dating them. As we come to be more familiar with early photographs we may, incidentally, come to interpret their subjects more aptly. We distinguish between the Sunday best of the formal portrait and the everyday reality of the snapshot, and we recognise that Victorian sternness may owe as much to the conditions of the photographer's studio as to an unrelievedly solemn habit of mind.

In its attempt to polish the window between ourselves and the past, this book looks briefly at the early history of photography, then moves on to consider the identification of the photographs we have inherited and the possibilities of dating them. Later sections deal briefly with related photographic items and with copying and caring for early photographs. The bibliography is selective, but points to possibilities for those who wish to pursue the subject further.

The Beginnings of Photography

The Effects of Light

The origins of photography lie in two sciences: optics and chemistry.

Optically, the ancestor of photography is the camera obscura. The way in which light could form pinhole images seems to have been known to the scholars of ancient China, but the first published description of the camera obscura (literally: darkened room) was written by Giovanni Battista della Porta in 1558.

To gain an idea of the camera obscura, imagine a closed, darkened room. One interior wall is painted white, and a pinhole is made in the opposite wall. In good light, a picture of the scene outside the room appears, upside down, on the white wall. This image can be turned the right way up, made brighter and defined more clearly by the use of a lens instead of a pinhole. This, in essence, is the camera obscura, which captured light's ability to form images.

Light can also have chemical effects. It can work on some materials to make them paler, as testified by the faded spines of books on shelves which catch the sunlight. This action of sunlight was an important ingredient in the early bleaching industry. Conversely, some materials darken in the sun's rays, as is firmly understood by the heliotropic and self-basting thousands who flock to the beach each summer. For some two hundred years before photography it was known that silver salts (now known as silver halides) darken when exposed to light. What was not possible, until the nineteenth century, was the ability to control and, when necessary, arrest this darkening process.

Prehistory

In the years which followed della Porta's account, the camera obscura underwent modifications. By the use of mirrors, the image could be directed away from the white wall and on to a sheet of paper, where it could then be traced. What worked with a darkened room could work with a darkened box, so a portable camera obscura became a possibility. When the screen on which the image fell was made of translucent paper or ground glass, the image could be seen from outside the box. Thus the camera obscura came to be seen as an aid to artists, especially in their struggles to master perspective. Further experiments with mirrors and lenses and, in particular, the invention of a movable lens tube to permit focussing, all helped to refine the device, so that by the end of the 17th century the basic camera already existed. What was lacking, and what would stay lacking for another 150 years, was the ability to preserve the image rather than to simply trace it.

It was to attempts to solve this problem that a knowledge of the chemical effects of light was eventually applied. The first recorded attempt to produce photographic images, described by Sir Humphrey Davey in 1802, was carried out by Thomas Wedgewood at the end of the 18th century. By placing objects upon materials treated with silver salts, Wedgewood was able to obtain images. Where the light hit the sensitised material, the surface darkened; where the object blocked out the light, the surface remained pale. Unfortunately, Wedgewood was unable to neutralise the sensitivity and fix his images and was, therefore, unable to view them by daylight. The next steps would be to use a light-sensitised material as the image-receiving screen in a camera, and to halt the chemical process so that the resulting picture could be retained.

The Earliest Photograph

The first person to combine the optical properties of light with its chemical effects and then preserve the result was Joseph Nicéphore Nièpce, a veteran of Napoleon's army. By 1827, after some years of trying, Nièpce managed to produce reasonably successful fixed pictures of a courtyard view taken from his attic window. After experimenting with the use of silver salts, he turned to the use of bitumen of Judea, a light-sensitive asphalt-like substance which was used in lithography. A plate of polished pewter was coated with varnish containing bitumen of Judea and exposed in a camera. Where affected by light, the bitumen hardened and turned pale. The remaining, unhardened varnish, corresponding to the dark areas of the image, was then washed off with a solvent of petroleum to re-expose the metal beneath. The picture was thus made up of pale hardened areas and patches of bare pewter. The contrast could then be improved by treatment with iodine vapour, which further darkened the metal.

A picture of Nièpce's courtyard survives, and the result is a faint pattern of light and shade with very little definition. It also took an eight hour exposure to the light to produce. Photography had started, but it still had far to go, and these early efforts were not enough to capture the popular imagination or to create an industry.

The Daguerrotype

One man who was impressed by Nièpce's work was Louis Daguerre, a scene-painter and the owner of the Paris Diorama. He sought out Nièpce and, in 1829, went into partnership with him. The process which he developed over the following ten years was rather different from that pioneered by his colleague, and Nièpce died in 1833 before he could see their joint effort brought to its successful conclusion.

On 7th January 1839 the Director of the Paris Observatory announced to the world that Daguerre had devised a method of fixing a reproduced image. The invention was called, with justifiable pride, the "daguerrotype".

Daguerre's method was to cover a copper plate with a thin coating of silver. The plate, having been highly polished, was then treated with iodine, the fumes of which worked on the silvered surface to produce a light-sensitive layer of silver iodide (or iodine of silver, as it was then known). The plate was exposed in a camera and the image then brought out by the action of mercury vapour. The problem of stopping the chemical action and fixing the image was at first solved by the use of common salt, but Daguerre quickly turned to the use of hypo, which was promoted as a fixing agent later in the same year, and of which more will be said in due course.

The resulting daguerrotype was essentially a negative image – the light parts of the original scene appeared dark on the silvered plate. But just as a modern black and white negative can appear positive when viewed at the right angle, so could the daguerrotype. The picture, though faint, was remarkably well defined.

The early daguerrotypes had their limitations. Exposures of ten minutes or more were necessary, and in less than ideal light over half an hour was occasionally needed. Scenes could be captured, because scenery stood still. People or horses passing by showed up as no more than a blur, and clocks appeared to have only hour hands. But as others took up the process, it was improved. Antoine Claudet and Richard Beard discovered that bromine acted as an accelerator, speeding up the rate at which chemicals reacted to light, and this led to exposure times being reduced to one or two minutes in the early 1840s. Portraits were now possible, and that possibility was very quickly explored and turned into a reality.

The Calotype

When Daguerre's process was announced, William Henry Fox Talbot was not delighted, for he too had been working on ways of making camera images permanent, and had achieved successful results as early as 1835. Frustrated by his own attempts at sketching, Fox Talbot had, on returning from his honeymoon tour of Europe, settled down at his Lacock Abbey home to tackle the same problems as Daguerre was working on. His solution was rather different.

Fox Talbot used paper rather than metal as the basis for his photographic plate. His earliest work followed on from that of Wedgewood. First, he brushed sheets of writing paper with a weak solution of salt, then soaked them in a strong solution of silver nitrate. He then placed such items as leaves, lace, flowers and feathers on the treated paper and exposed object and paper to sunlight. Where light reached the paper, through holes in lace or gaps between leaves as well as on the outer, uncovered areas, the sensitised surface turned dark. Where the object itself prevented light from reaching it, the paper remained white. Talbot called these pictures "photogenic drawings". From here it was but a short step to using the treated paper as the plate in a camera.

The product so far of Fox Talbot's process was a negative image, with the light parts of the original subject showing dark on the picture. But he realised that positives could be made by placing the negative over a second sheet of treated paper. Light would filter through the pale parts of the negative and darken the paper beneath, thus reversing the blacks and whites, and producing an image in which the light values were those of the subject.

For his very earliest pictures, Fox Talbot used potassium iodide as the fixing agent, but this gave a yellowish quality to the highlights, and he quickly changed to the use of common salt solution, which acted by converting any remaining light-sensitive silver nitrate to non-sensitive silver chloride. This method, too, produced a colour cast, with the white parts of the picture taking on a pale lilac tint within a few hours of fixing.

Although Fox Talbot's earliest pictures dated from 1835, he had published nothing about his discoveries until the announcement of Daguerre's success in 1839 stole his thunder and stung him into action. He now acted quickly, and on the last day of January read a paper about his process to the Royal Society.

At first his exposures took half an hour or more, but in 1840 he discovered the existence of a latent image which was capable of development. An exposure of between one and three minutes could produce an invisible image on the prepared paper, and this, given the appropriate chemical treatment, could be brought out after the picture had been taken. His developer (or "exciting liquid" as he first called it) was gallic acid, and it had the incidental effect of improving the picture's quality.

By 1841 Fox Talbot was ready to patent his method, with gallic acid as the chemical accelerator. He called his improved process the "calotype" and marketed licences for its use. The licences were only taken up by about a dozen people, and the following years were marked by some legal wrangling over patents into which crept an understandable degree of bitterness on Fox Talbot's part. But amongst those who bought a licence were David Octavius Hill and Robert Adamson, who set up in partnership in Edinburgh in 1843. Their initial aim was to provide portrait studies to help Hill, a painter, in the mammoth task of creating a picture to commemorate the first assembly of the Free Church of Scotland. They went on to take a series of impressive portraits during the few years before Adamson's death at the age of 26 in 1848.

During his lifetime, Fox Talbot made a series of improvements to the calotype process, including the waxing of the negative paper to make it more translucent, and the use of hypo as a fixing agent. Warmer tones were achieved by the inclusion of dilute nitric acid in the treatment used for the printing paper. The latent image principle was not used for the printing stage of the process, since, once the negative had been produced, time was no longer of the essence. For a while some applied the name of "Talbotype" to the process, but Talbot himself had never promoted this, and it was his term, "Calotype", which stuck.

Although in 1839 Fox Talbot was too late to prevent Daguerre from reaping the glory of being first in the field, and although both men's processes were soon to become obsolete, it is now possible to see Fox Talbot as the true progenitor of photography as we know it today, for it was his method which pointed the way forward. It was he who produced a negative-positive method which made possible multiple copies rather than the one-off image of the daguerrotype, and it was he whose work with the latent image set the agenda for later developments.

The earliest surviving photographic negative is of a window in Fox Talbot's home at Lacock Abbey. The home, with its attached photographic museum, can still be visited, though National Trust regulations now prevent the homage-inclined photographer from recording the window from an indoor viewpoint.

Hypo

1839 was very much the year for important announcements. Shortly after Daguerre and Fox Talbot had made their successes public, Sir John Herschel announced the use of hypo, or sodium thiosulphate, as a fixative. Herschel, a close friend of Fox Talbot, had discovered in 1819 that hypo dissolved silver salts, and so was immediately able to apply this knowledge to the search for a satisfactory fixing agent. By dissolving any light-sensitive silver salts which remained on the plate, negative or print, hypo rendered the surface stable and prevented any further reaction to light. Hypo was quickly adopted for fixing both daguerrotypes and calotypes, and was to go on to prove its worth with subsequent processes.

Whilst it is for hypo that Herschel is best known in the photographic field, it should be said that he also discovered the blueprint process, which was not to be taken up seriously until much later in the century, and devised a method for using treated glass rather than paper as the basis for a photograph. Because of the fragility of glass and the difficulties of handling it, Herschel and Fox Talbot both put this idea aside until rather later. Herschel also had an abiding influence on the language of photography, for the terms "positive", "negative" and "snapshot" were all coined by him.

The Wet Collodion Process

Though Herschel and Fox Talbot did not persevere with the use of glass, Frederick Scott Archer employed it in what was to be perhaps the most important step forward of the age. In March 1851 he introduced his wet collodion process, which used glass negatives to produce paper prints. The method was faster than those which preceded it: a transparent glass plate negative could produce a print in a quarter of the time required for one made of waxed paper. Glass was also better as a negative because it did away with the textured, grainy effect which resulted from the fibrous structure of paper. The new process, therefore, found immediate favour with the professional photographer. It came into widespread use, portrait studios appeared all over the world and even the dedicated amateur felt able to take up the activity as a hobby.

Yet this immense popularity arose in spite of the cumbersome nature of the process, for making wet collodion pictures was a major undertaking.

Collodion was gun-cotton dissolved in ether. It dried to create an airtight film and was used in hospitals to dress wounds. Whilst this drying property was invaluable in hospital, it caused a considerable problem for the photographer, who had to work with the sticky substance while it was still wet, and before the light-sensitive silver salts that were mixed into it were sealed in and rendered ineffective. The glass plate was coated in collodion which was allowed to become tacky. Then it was dipped into a bath of silver nitrate and used immediately. Once the plate had been exposed, and before the coating had time to dry, the latent image was developed, using pyro-gallic acid. The resulting negative could then be used to produce a positive print by laying it over sensitised paper and exposing again to the light. Alternatively, the glass negative, if deliberately thin and underexposed, could be placed against a black background to produce a one-off finished picture known as a glass collodion positive, or, more commonly, an ambrotype.

The complications of wet-collodion processing proved to be no great deterrent, and portable wet-collodion darkrooms were carried all over the world by a whole generation of early landscape and documentary photographers. It is to this process that we owe the pictorial records of the Crimean War and the American Civil War. Amateurs, too, used the method. One of them, C.L. Dodgson ("Lewis Carroll"), commented on it in his parody of Longfellow:

"Secondly my Hiawatha
Made with cunning hand a mixture
Of the acid pyrogallic,
And of glacial acetic
And of alcohol and water."

He made fun of the process, but he used it with enthusiasm.

Egg Whites and After

The standard printing paper for use with wet collodion negatives was known as albumen paper. Albumen paper was introduced by Blanquart Everard in 1850. Paper with an albumen coating was treated with salt and silver nitrate, then exposed beneath a glass negative until the picture appeared. The majority of prints made between 1850 and 1890 were made on albumen paper from wet-collodion negatives. By 1866 it was estimated that in Britain alone six million egg whites a year were being used in the preparation of photographic paper, and as late as 1894 a firm in Dresden, Europe's largest producer of albumen paper, was using up some six thousand eggs a day.

Because albumen prints had a tendency to become yellow and fade, other printing processes were sought and found. Sir Joseph Wilson Swan introduced carbon prints in 1864, and the same decade saw the development of W.B. Woodbury's "Woodburytype", a process which came to be used widely for pasted-in book illustrations in the 1870s. Both processes achieved greater permanence of pigment, and both met with some success, but neither managed to supplant the popular albumen print.

The first natural colour photograph was produced by James Clark Maxwell in 1861, but more than thirty years were to pass before effective use was made of his method.

Eventually though, in the 1890s, albumen paper was superseded by gelatine-chloride printing-out papers, which were faster to react, cheaper to buy and far less liable to fading. The day of the egg white was over, but not before it had dominated photographic printing for forty years.

The Rise of the Professional Photographer

London's first professional studio was opened by Richard Beard, the improver of the daguerrotype, in the early 1840s, and other daguerrotype photographers quickly followed. There was no comparable growth in calotype studios, for licensees of the process were few, and a minority of those who practised it sought to make their living by it.

The primary requirement of the early studios was light, and large areas of window were a common feature. These windows generally faced north to avoid the unflattering effects that direct sunlight can produce, such as shadows beneath the nose. In winter or in poor weather opening hours were likely to be curtailed. Not surprisingly, studios were often set up on the top floor of the premises or in a glass-house on the roof. In rooftop studios the subject might be placed in a chair set on a revolving platform which could be turned as the day wore on, to make the most of the changing light. Blue-tinted glass was often used in such studios, since it reduced the glare for the subject, whilst having no adverse effects on the end product.

That the sitters should so often appear stiff and unsmiling is not difficult to understand, since they were required to sit perfectly still, helped perhaps by a head-clamp or brace, for one or two long minutes. Let those who think two minutes short try sitting motionless for that time, blinking as little as possible. If that proves easy, let them do it again whilst trying to maintain a charming and natural smile.

Whilst the daguerrotypes gained great popularity amongst those who could afford them, it was the patent-free wet-collodion process that made possible the real rise, in the 1850s, of the commercial photographer. Even more important was the boost given by the introduction of the carte de visite in the mid-fifties. This visiting-card-sized photograph became a craze, for crazes are nothing new. Once royalty had patronised a carte photographer, the demand became immense and the price dropped. Before the introduction of the carte, photographic portraits could cost two or three pounds, which was twice the weekly income of many ordinary families. The carte arrived on the scene at half-a-crown and soon dropped to a shilling. Suddenly photographs were within the range of the common man and not just an indulgence of the portrait-painted classes.

So professional photography boomed. Photographers set up in every town, and some towns had many. Glasshouse Street, just off Picadilly Circus, is said to have gained its name from the large number of photographic studios in the area. The 1851 census showed 51 commercial photographers in the country; by 1861 the number had risen to 2,534. The phenomenon may perhaps be compared to the rapid spread of video-hire shops in more recent years.

Of course, with the increase in practitioners came something of a fall in standards. Certainly, the East End photographers described by Henry Mayhew, in his investigation of Victorian London, seem to have produced pictures that were as unrecognisable as they were unappealing. But the photographically serious-minded tend to turn their noses up at the smaller and more provincial studios generally, arguing that popularisation led to vulgarisation. The family historian, however, might reasonably feel that without popularisation, and possibly vulgarisation, few of us would now possess likenesses of our Victorian forebears.

One passing titbit of improbable information deserves a mention. Victorian photographers, when shorter exposures became possible, apparently encouraged ladies to say not "cheese" but "prunes". Presumably the choice of word was designed to produce on the sitter's face a not unattractive moue. When one examines photographs of the time, however, it has to be admitted that the incidence of not unattractive moues is by no means high.

Dry Plates

The inconvenience of wet collodion left much room for improvement, and the need was for a dry plate process. Yet, paradoxically, the popularity of wet collodion meant that a new method would not easily catch on.

In fact, a dry collodion process emerged in 1855 and by 1860 dry plates were on sale in England, but they failed to make a major impact. Not until 1871, when Dr Richard Leach Maddox of Southampton published his method of preparing gelatin dry plates, did a shift in loyalties begin. By 1873 John Burgess was marketing the new plates, but even then the change was slow. Dry plates were more expensive at first, since, unlike wet collodion plates, they could not be scraped clean and re-used. As the seventies progressed, however, Maddox's process began to establish itself more firmly.

Maddox had developed a coating which was compounded of cadmium bromide, silver nitrate and gelatin, and which retained its sensitivity to light when dry. As well as being easier to use, his plates were kinder to cameras, the materials of which tended to rot as a result of frequent contact with the damp and sticky collodion coatings. The new plates were factory made, were easy to store and did not have to be prepared in the field. These features all allowed greater mobility to the outdoor photographer.

Perhaps the decisive factor in the shift to new methods was the discovery in 1878 by Charles Bennet that leaving the emulsion to brew for a day or two at 90° Fahrenheit, before spreading it on the plate, led to greatly increased light sensitivity. Suddenly it was possible to take photographs with exposures of as little as one twenty-fifth of a second.

This development speeded up the change, and by 1885 wet collodion was obsolete. With it went all the equipment needed for on-the-spot treatment of plates. Photography had gained enormously in convenience, and the age of the snapshot was just around the corner.

The Arrival of the Snapshot

Further improvements in photography now needed a lighter and more flexible film base to replace the weighty and fragile glass. Celluloid had in fact been invented in 1861 by Alexander Parkes, but it was not at first made in the clear, thin and flexible sheets that would render it suitable for photographic use. In 1888 John Carbutt of Philadelphia began to produce celluloid in such a form. What was then required was somebody to see its possibilities as a film base.

George Eastman was to be that man. In 1885 he invented a form of gelatin-coated, paper-backed film, which could be used in a roll in a specially designed camera, and from which the paper could be discarded when the film was ready for processing. He designed a purpose-built box camera in which to use the film and began to market this in 1889 as the No. 1 Kodak. The name "Kodak", incidentally, had no specific connotations; like the camera which it identified, it was invented for international use. The Kodak took circular pictures, 2½" in diameter, about a hundred to a roll. The secret of Eastman's success lay in what happened when the film had been exposed. The film was sealed in the camera, and the customer had simply to return the entire apparatus to the Eastman factory, where the film was removed and processed. The company then returned the camera, reloaded and ready for use, together with the set of prints. Eastman's slogan, "You press the button and we do the rest", summed up the procedure perfectly. Success was immediate. The camera was easy to use and quickly became popular. But further developments were to come, which were to help the Eastman company to become, in the 1890s, the biggest photographic firm in the world.

By 1890 Eastman had realised the possibilities of celluloid, and he shifted to this material for his films, producing rolls capable of giving a more manageable 12 or 24 prints. 100 prints to a film may seem like good value, but it takes a long time before the results of the earlier exposures see the light of day, and photographers have never been great believers in deferred gratification. In 1895 he introduced a black paper packaging, which facilitated loading and unloading outside a darkened room. Then, in 1900, came the greatest step of all towards the popularisation of photography – the box Brownie. The Brownie was named after pixie-like characters in a popular series of children's stories, and a frog-faced brownie, taking a photograph, illustrated the packaging in which the cameras were sold. It is sobering to think that, had the invention of snapshot photography been delayed, the world might have been faced with the Box Bambi, or even, the heavens forfend, the Box Barbie.

The Brownie cost a mere dollar, and within a year 100,000 were sold. Amateurs everywhere were taking their own pictures without having to be chemists. There were, of course, those who resented the intrusiveness of the box camera, such as those gentlemen who threatened to thrash the cads who haunted beaches to take pictures of women in bathing suits. But there were far more people who used the new cameras than there were people who objected to them. In 1860, talking of future possibilities, Herschel had coined the word "snapshot". He had died a few years before he could see his vision become a reality, but now the era of the snapshot had arrived.

Glass plate cameras did not disappear. They continued to be used by professionals and serious amateurs well into the new century. But photography was now available to Everyman. Eastman had removed, at a stroke, the deterrent complications of photography, and this, as much as the low price, was a breakthrough. Many people wanted, and still want, their photography made easy. It is not an unreasonable request, for their interest is in the end product rather than the process. Indeed, today's disposable cameras are simply a revival of Eastman's brilliant marketing idea. Plus, as they say, ça change. . . . .

Identifying Early Photographs

Whilst many variations on the photographic process and products were tried before the First World War, the kinds of photograph most likely to be encountered are relatively few, and usually a fair attempt can be made to identify what they are. For this, some knowledge of the characteristics of each type is needed, including, often, an awareness of the ways in which different kinds of photograph have deteriorated.

Daguerrotypes and Calotypes

Daguerrotypes and calotypes are the least likely kinds of photograph to be found in the family archive, since they date from before the major boom in commercial photography. Both processes were relatively expensive, and both had their share of failures. At first the long exposure times meant that neither was thought of as particularly suitable for portraiture. Soon, of course, exposure times were reduced, and daguerrotype portrait studios were opened up. Calotype photographers never really explored the commercial market, though of their number Hill and Adamson must still rank amongst the great portrait photographers, and lucky are any family historians whose ancestors were among their Edinburgh gentry or Newhaven fisherfolk subjects. Compared to the later users of the wet collodion process, practitioners of both daguerrotype and calotype were few, though, statistically, there has to be a far greater chance of inheriting a daguerrotype than a calotype.

The daguerrotype was much admired for its precision of detail, though the image was faint, and the highly polished, mirror-like surface made it impossible to view from all angles. Since the daguerrotype is essentially a treated negative, the image is reversed, as an examination of buttoned garments may show. It may be evident that the coating is of silver. But a golden toning is also quite likely, for the image was often gilded with a solution of gold salt to soften the cold, metallic look. There is also a possibility of the metal being tarnished, especially around the edges of the picture. The surface is very fragile, and the slightest abrasions leave a scratch or scar.

Since the surface is so vulnerable, it is usually protected by glass and is often presented in a small frame or case, such as had previously been used for miniature paintings. The cases are often of leather, opening like a book, with a velvet lining facing the picture.

The calotype was capable of much more subtle tonal effects but was likely to be less sharply defined. A calotype is printed on paper from a paper negative, and the fact that the negative was a fibrous substance means that the end product may have a grainy quality, with poor reproduction of fine detail. As a rough guide, calotype portraits are most likely to measure between 4" and 5" one way and 6" and 7" the other. The surface is matt, with a very faint sheen. The colour is reddish brown or sepia, but fading is very likely, especially at the edges, when the result is a yellowish colour. Finally, it should again be emphasised that calotypes, in particular, are rare.

Ambrotypes

Ambrotypes, wet collodion negatives turned into one-off positives, have something of the elegance and quality of daguerrotypes and came to fill the niche that they left. But they were cheaper to produce, coincided with the rise of the commercial photographer, and have, therefore, come down to us in much greater numbers.

The ambrotype was devised by Scott Archer in collaboration with Peter Fry. It took for its starting point a thin, underexposed glass negative. This pale image on clear glass was then given a backing of black velvet or black shellac. The result of this, when viewed from the unmasked side, was to turn the clear glass areas black. Against this black background the exposed parts of the negative, which, though darker than clear glass, were silvery, reflected the light. Thus a positive effect was achieved. It appears that sometimes the exposed parts of the negative were chemically bleached before the black backing was added. This would certainly make for greater contrast, but authorities differ in their accounts of the process and it is difficult to be sure how widespread this refinement was. Though some ambrotypes do tend to be sombre, many show good contrast of light and shade which it is hard to believe mere backing of an otherwise untreated, though thin, negative would produce.

These pictures were originally known in Britain as collodion positives, but they were patented in the United States under the name of ambrotype, which is how they soon came to be generally known.

An ambrotype has those features which are characteristic of wet collodion pictures in general: the image is sharp and clear, and more reminiscent of the daguerrotype than the calotype. There may, though, as already indicated, be a dullness about the highlights. Whereas with a daguerrotype it is necessary to find the right angle for viewing, no such difficulty is presented by the ambrotype. On the other hand, when the picture is moved about in relation to the light, it is often possible to find a point at which a negative effect is created.

It was common to touch up details of an ambrotype with a hint of colour for lips or cheeks, or with a spot of gilding for such items as buttons, jewellery and watch chains. These cosmetic refinements may still often be found, though the colouring may well have faded somewhat with the passage of time.

If the black backing has been applied to the emulsion side of the plate, then one views the picture from the back of the original negative and, as on a positive, such things as buttoned garments appear the right way round. If this has been done, in theory no additional glass is needed at the front of the picture, since the thickness of the plate provides its own protection. In practice, however, a sheet of protective glass seems generally to have been included in frames and cases, whichever side of the original is black-backed. Alternatively, the black backing could be on the untreated side of the negative, to allow a clearer image. In such cases, the picture is reversed. In such cases, too, it is often possible to see the white parts of the pictures standing out a little from the dark parts, because the thickness of the plate separates the pale, chemically activated emulsion from the black backing.

Although sizes up to full plate (6½″ × 8½″) are possible for ambrotypes, they are generally considerably smaller, with 2¼″ × 3¼″ being quite common.

Certain signs of deterioration are diagnostic features when it comes to identifying ambrotypes. The black shellac backing, which seems to have been more commonly used than velvet, has proved liable to crazing and flaking. Sometimes small areas of shellac have fallen away to leave patches of clear glass; sometimes a mosaic pattern of white cracks can be seen in the darker areas of the picture. A further kind of deterioration is the result of moisture invasion between the layers of the packaged end product, and this can show itself, especially near the edges, as small mould growths or water ring-marks.

Like daguerrotypes, ambrotypes are frequently found framed or cased, and since cases in general, and one type of case in particular, are so often associated with ambrotypes, it is appropriate to consider the matter of their packaging. A sandwich was generally made of picture and protective glass, perhaps with a thin metal matt or decorative border between, and this was bound around the edges with a thin strip of paper or tape to inhibit moisture invasion. The sandwich was then fitted into a thin metal mount or frame, and this in turn was fitted into one side of a hinged case. The other face of the opened case commonly held a plush velvet lining, but a second, companion picture was also a possibility.

The metal used for early matts and frames was often brass, but during the ambrotype period pinchbeck was generally used. This was a soft, brass-like, gold-coloured alloy that was produced in thin sheets, which could be cut to size, and from which the holes in frames could be stamped out. The overlapping edges of pinchbeck frames could be folded over the edges of the glass behind.

The case itself, during the daguerrotype period, was most frequently of leather, but with the cheaper ambrotypes, cheaper materials came into use, and wood, paper, papier mache and leathercloth were all used. One particular material, however, tends to be associated with ambrotype cases, and that is thermoplastic. In 1854 Samuel Rich patented the Union Case, made of a plastic material compounded of shellac and sawdust. This American invention was, in fact, the first commercial use of plastic. Because the thermoplastic was capable of being moulded, it could be used to make highly decorated products, and by the 1860s very ornate Union Cases were produced, decorated with flowers, fruits, scrolls, swags and even bas-relief pictures. The Union Case came to be particularly associated with ambrotypes. Because of the date of its introduction, it is tempting to assert that if a picture is in a Union Case, it cannot be a daguerrotype, but there is always the possibility of a photograph of one period being later transferred to a case of a more recent date.

Cartes de Visite

In 1853 André Disderi, a Parisian photographer, had the idea of making several small exposures on one large photographic plate. The practice did not catch on at first until, so the story goes, Napoleon III stopped off at Disderi's studio, when leading his troops to war with Austria, in order to have his likeness taken. This show of imperial approval led to a quick and lively interest in Disderi and his photographs. In Britain a similar boost was given to the new size of photographs when Queen Victoria and Prince Albert permitted John Mayall to photograph them in carte format at Buckingham Palace. The resulting portraits were published in book form, but it was as individual cartes that they found an eager and enormous market. Everybody wanted cartes of the royal family and, soon, of famous people generally. Not only that – everybody wanted to appear on cartes themselves.

Originally intended and used as illustrated calling cards, the cartes quickly became desirable objects in their own right. People began to collect them, snapping up likenesses of celebrities and swapping pictures with their friends. The craze was known as cartomania. There is, incidentally, a note of warning to be sounded here for family historians. The appearance of an eminent Victorian or two in a family collection of cartes does not necessarily imply any kinship or even acquaintance. They are no more likely to be relations than are the cut-out magazine posters of pop stars stuck on the bedroom walls of today's young.

As the craze developed, specially produced albums were created for keeping the pictures in, with carte-sized apertures ready and waiting. The albums could then be displayed to friends and relations and were, in effect, the coffee table books of their age. It is to the carte that we owe the invaluable institution of the famiy album.

Once the idea of cartes was firmly taken up, special cameras were produced, generally designed to take eight pictures on a single plate. Some had a simple lens, taking a series of shots on a plate which was shifted into a new position between exposures. Others had multiple lenses which operated simultaneously. Still others had multiple lenses, but took pictures one after another. The survival of two identical prints does not, of course, have to mean that a simultaneous exposure camera was used, since negatives allowed as many copies to be made from a picture as were needed.

The identification of cartes is simple. The paper picture, normally an albumen print, measures about 3½″ × 2¼″ and is brought to a size of about 4″ × 2½″ by being pasted on a slightly larger photographer's trade card, which usually bears his or her name and address, and often additional advertising matter. The complete item is about the size of the visiting card from which it derives its name. The only type of photograph that could be confused with a carte is the tintype, since this was sometimes made up to the same finished size so that it could be included in the standard albums. Of tintypes more will be said in due course.

Cabinet Prints

Although cartes continued to be popular until the end of the 19th century, sales dropped off from the enormous and unsustainable peak of the early 1860s, and to counter this a new and larger size of popular portrait, the cabinet print, was introduced in 1866. Though they never reached the heights of success achieved by their smaller relations in the days of cartomania, the cabinet prints proved and remained very popular, and many of them survive.

As cabinet prints took over a large corner of the portrait market, photographic albums were produced with spaces of the right size to house them, or, perhaps more commonly, with some spaces of cabinet size and some of carte size.

Like cartes, cabinet prints are easy to identify. The recipe is the same, but on a larger scale: a paper print is pasted on a slightly larger photographer's card. The size of prints varies a little but is generally around 4″ × 5½″, and the finished item comes to about 4½″ × 6½″. Albumen prints are the most usual, at least until the later years of the century.

Printing Processes

Since albumen paper has been mentioned as the most commonly used for cartes de visite and cabinet prints, some attempt to describe it seems in order. The problem is that many different processes were tried in Victorian and Edwardian times, and descriptions of their results are not always illuminating. Descriptions so often have to depend largely on colour, and the perception of colour is highly subjective. Various kinds of print have been variously described as reddish brown, warm brown, sepia, rich brown, dark brown, chocolate brown and blackish brown. Unfortunately, one man's reddish brown is another man's sepia. Or even the same man's sepia. So although these pages have already been very occasionally guilty of reference to colour, and are about to incur further guilt, such references are of limited use, and there is no intention here of wading very far into the fraught field of identifying processes. Fortunately, since albumen prints dominated for so long in the most popular fields of portraiture, there is little need to venture far, though any reader with an inclination to learn more is referred to "Family History in Focus", mentioned in the bibliography, where expert guidance is offered by braver and better men.

The albumen print, which caused a huge consumption of egg whites already referred to, is smooth surfaced and slightly glossy in its finish. It is fragile and easily creased, which is why pasting it to a piece of stout card was such a suitable practice. Its natural colour is sepia, but there is a yellowish tone, which becomes very pronounced as the print fades, and which was considered unattractive. The prints were often, therefore, treated with gold chloride to give a richer tone which is often referred to as plum coloured. This treatment also increased the "permanence" of the image.

For better quality cartes and cabinets the carbon print was sometimes used. This process was introduced in 1864 and was still being used until about 1930. It gave strong, rich colours and good gradation of tones. As well as the usual sepia range, carbon printing could produce results that were black, blue, green and chalk red. There, at least, are some colours which leave little room for argument, and which may serve to identify some carbon prints. For those in the brown/sepia range the problem remains, but help in identification can be gained from the fact that carbon prints, when viewed at an angle, have a slight relief effect, almost as if the image has been painted on. As well as being used on some cartes and cabinets, carbon printing is often found on photographs made on materials other than paper, and most prints on a non-paper base made between about 1870 and 1915 were produced by this process.

Tintypes

Cheapest of all portraits was the tintype, or ferrotype as it was more properly if less popularly called, since the photographic plate was a small piece of iron. The process was patented by an American, Hamilton L. Smith, in the mid 1850s, and involved coating a thin, blackened sheet of iron with a wet collodion emulsion. The system was developed for the use of the itinerant photographer, with all the chemical operations taking place inside a specially designed camera. The cameras were multi-lensed and could give up to 36 exposures on one plate. The plate was processed quickly, taken from the camera, cut up into individual tintypes and handed, still wet, to the customer. The cost was only a few pence and the result, as with daguerrotypes and ambrotypes, was a unique picture, though the quality was much inferior.

At their simplest, tintypes may be recognised from the fact that they are on a thin, sharp-edged piece of metal, but this fact may be disguised by a frame or mount. If, though mounted or framed, the picture's surface is not covered by glass, a light tap with the back of the fingernail will demonstrate that it is not a paper print, (though whether such treatment of old pictures can be responsibly recommended is another question). The image is reversed and likely to be of poor quality. Though some examples have good contrast, many have a murky appearance, for black and the darker shades of grey were what the tintype was really good at. In theory the picture can be of any size, but small predominates, since most tintypes are merely snipped-off fractions of a whole plate. Many measure no more than 1½″ × 2½″. The picture is often slipped into a card and paper mount to bring it up to carte size for insertion into an album.

Sometimes the metal seems to have been very thinly coated with the emulsion, which by now has worn down in places to the bare metal. These examples are particularly vulnerable to scratching. Other tintypes seem to have been more thickly coated, but this can result in bubbles (or popped bubbles) on the surface, and in tiny wrinkles which may sometimes be the result of the picture having been touched before it was properly dry.

Like other one-off portraits, the tintype is sometimes framed, though a cheaper quality is evident both in the papery materials of the outer casing, if there is one, and in the pinchbeck, which may appear thin and roughly cut. Some survive in the form of glass and tintype sandwich, held together by the folded-over edges of the pinchbeck frame. In these cases, the metal back can be clearly seen.

One particular variation was the gem tintype, the smallest portrait which was commercially produced. This measured a mere 1″ × ½″ and was either mounted in a cut-out space in a carte-sized mount or kept in a locket or brooch.

It is easy to disparage the humble tintype. The fact remains that it extended even further the range of classes covered by early photography, and even with people who were also photographed by other methods, it can show them in a different setting. Since the tintype was very much the province of the travelling photographer, it can show our ancestors away from the formality of a studio, as they appeared, say, on a day's outing at the seaside or at the fair.

Novelties

From time to time various new sizes or materials enjoyed a degree of popularity, though none can be considered a major milestone in the history of photography.

Pictures where the novelty lay in their shape can be recognised from their measurements, and tend towards rectangles of a more elongated kind than usual. Promenade Prints, measuring 7" × 4", were introduced in 1875; Boudoir Prints, of uncertain date, were 8½" × 5¼". In the early years of the twentieth century Panel Prints were something of a vogue. These 5¼" × 1¾" narrow upright rectangles cornered a share of the postcard market for pictures of actresses. There is some room for confusion here, though, as Panel Print was also used as a name for rather larger mounted pictures of 8¼" × 4". Another Edwardian format, the Coupon Print, came as a strip of upright rectangles, each 3½ · 1½". Few of these novelties are likely to survive as family portraits.

Tintypes are sometimes found as circular exposures, though the metal on which they are printed is cut up into conventional rectangular pieces. Sometimes photographs were given the appearance of round or oval shape by being mounted in the shaped aperture of a card designed to fit into a carte or cabinet print album.

Photographs incorporated into jewellery, especially lockets, were popular in both Victorian and Edwardian times, and these were often hand-tinted. Some jewellery photographs are gem tintypes, but many are small paper prints cut down to the right size and shape.

Non-standard materials were also tried as the photographic base. Portraits on porcelain and glassware were popular in the later nineteenth and early twentieth centuries, and pictures on enamel plaques were in some favour from 1880 until after the Great War. Cloth and wood were also used, but these were often for subjects other than people.

Of the novelty materials used for portraiture, opal glass is particularly attractive. Such pictures were valued and produced in some numbers from 1865 until about the turn of the century. Various processes were used, of which carbon printing was the most common, especially in the later years. These photographs are liable to be of cabinet print size or larger. If they are framed, they may be identified by the white, opalescent appearance of the background and probably by the characteristics, already mentioned, of a carbon print. If they are unframed, the white, translucent glass is, of course, easy to recognise. Whilst the print itself may have stood up well to the passage of time, the glass may have taken on a yellowish or buff mottling.

Roll Film Pictures

Very early forms of roll film were made of oiled, sensitised paper or gelatin emulsion, with a paper backing from which it was later stripped off for processing. But it was with celluloid roll film that snapshot photography really took off, and with the box Brownie that it became fully the activity of Everyman. Thus, whilst roll film pictures could date from the last years of the nineteenth century, in practice we may reasonably think of them as a twentieth century phenomenon.

Size and shape can be of some use in identifying pictures made from roll film. The very earliest Kodaks took circular pictures, 2½" in diameter. The first Brownies took photographs that were 2¼" square, but within a couple of years the Number 2 Brownie was producing pictures 2¼" × 3¼". This size proved very popular and survived until about 1960. Shortly before the First World War the 127 roll film, with shots 2½" × 1⅝", was introduced for use in the Kodak Vest Pocket Camera, and this film too survived for use over many years in a variety of models of camera.

It may be that a set of old prints conveniently conforms to a familiar size, but there is every chance that it will not. New cameras gave different numbers of shots on old film, many different sizes of film were tried, and even as early as 1900 the enlarging of pictures was possible, though not yet common.

One obvious distinguishing feature of the snapshot is that it was taken outside. Admittedly, earlier kinds of portrait could be taken out-of-doors, and tintypes often were, but for the snapshot the open air was an essential fact of life. Serious amateurs might come to have their own indoor lighting set-up, with expensive floodlights, or home-made equipment with biscuit tins as reflectors. Later still, flash equipment came into common use, with a new bulb for each picture, and the juggling with hot, dead bulbs that one had taken out too quickly. But before the First World War, and, indeed, for the first fifty or so years of the century, snapshot photography relied almost entirely on bright, natural light. Thus holiday photos abound, but it is as if Christmas never happened. Not only were outdoor pictures in good sunlight the rule, but most photographers conscientiously kept the light behind them, so that the faces of hat-wearing subjects are shadowed by peaks and brims, and the rest of the world screws up its eyes against the glare of the sun.

Roll film pictures are also liable to display all the faults of later snapshot photographs, and some of them to a greater degree, since modern films are more tolerant of ill-judged exposures, and since many modern cameras make decisions that either used to be made by the operator or were simply not on offer for the making. At any rate, washed out or dark images abound. People are so far from the camera that they are scarcely recognisable. Horizons are tilted, scalps are cut off, subjects disappear from the side of the frame, trees appear to grow from heads. Of course, not all amateurs were amateurish, but if our forebears commonly made mistakes, they are only the mistakes that we have all imitated in our time. In short, then as now, snapshot pictures were prey to all the ills that celluloid is heir to.

Stereos

Stereoscopic photos, which, when looked at through a suitable viewer, gave the illusion of three dimensions, were perhaps photography's earliest craze, predating, though not reaching the same proportions as, cartomania. The very earliest of these pictures were produced by the daguerrotype process, but their first peak of popularity came in the 1850s and 1860s. Though they were rather eclipsed by the carte de visite, they enjoyed periodic revivals of popularity well into the next century. By about 1860 almost every middle-class Victorian household had a stereoscope and a collection of accompanying photographs, and an industry emerged to cater for their taste. The London Stereoscopic Company was one of the most successful firms to enter the market, and in the early 1860s, at the height of the craze, it boasted a publications list of some hundred thousand subjects.

The effect obtained by looking simultaneously at two pictures, representing the same scene from slightly differing viewpoints, had been discovered by Sir Charles Wheatstone before the age of photography. Photography was able to use this effect by means of a camera fitted with two lenses, which were placed the same distance apart as the human eyes.

That each eye, having its own field of vision, registers a slightly different scene, may be simply ascertained by closing first one and then the other. When these two scenes are viewed at the same time, that is to say, when both eyes are open, we see in three dimensions, judging not only breadth and height, but also the distance any object or part of an object is from the eyes. When we open both eyes, the effect may not immediately seem more three-dimensional than when we just open one, but a simple experiment will show that it is indeed on binocular vision that we rely for our judgement of depth or distance. Scatter a number of small coins on a table at about arm's length. Close one eye, decide on a coin, and place the end of a forefinger quickly over the centre of it. Try this a few times, changing hands and eyes, and moving the position of the coins frequently to prevent memory from compensating for any uncertainty of judgement. Because the items are so very close, most attempts will probably be successful, but there may well be a few near misses. Now repeat the procedure with both eyes open. The success rate in placing a finger-tip unhesitatingly on the centre of the chosen coin is likely to be greater. The difference between the monocular and binocular attempts may be small, since the objects are so near, but the chances are that the test will demonstrate that the accuracy of three-dimensional vision has much to do with having two eyes see almost, but not quite, the same thing.

What the eyes achieve naturally, the stereoscope imitates. When we use a viewer to look at the two slightly different stereo images side by side, simultaneously but independently, with the right eye seeing one picture and the left eye seeing the other, we recreate that divergence between images seen in real life by each eye.

It may at first seem that consideration of stereo pictures is of little interest to the family historian. Though pictures of people exist, stereos were not primarily or even significantly a medium for portraits. Pictures with more depth, where people, if included at all, are set against a background, were considered more appropriate for making the most of the stereoscopic effect. The chances, therefore, of finding a stereo picture of an ancestor are minimal. If inherited stereos are of interest, it may only be as family heirloooms. But there is the possibility that some of the scenes depicted are of significance. All manner of subjects were photographed, often taken as a series and sold as sets. There were natural history pictures, photographs of foot and paw prints to aid trackers, anatomical series showing skulls and the structure of the eye, and medical series featuring interesting prostheses. There were anecdotal pictures, stage-managed to tell a story or point a moral, and resembling stills from films. There were nude studies, which was one kind of portraiture where the three-dimensional effect might be considered of interest. But more than anything else, there were places: buildings of London, scenes along the Thames, famous cities, the sights of Russia. With stereoscopes our ancestors travelled the world. Many of these scenes were part of sets. But local pictures can also be found – the church, the town hall, the High Street – and certainly any inherited collection of cards should be checked for scenes that their owners were familiar with. Thus, though in a more modest way, stereos can have much the same sort of interest as topographical postcards for the historian who wishes to see the family in a context.

There is, of course, no difficulty in identifying stereos. They consist of two nearly identical pictures side by side. A few are daguerrotypes; most are prints, often albumen prints pasted on cards. These were viewed by reflected light. Some stereos are found on glass, and some on tissue inserted into holes in card. These types would be slotted into the open end of a viewer, and were thus lit from behind by transmitted light.

The size of stereos varies, but the cards for the most popular type of viewer measure about 7″ × 3½″, containing two pictures which are each about 3″ square.

Finally, since it is quite possible to inherit pictures without the accompanying viewer, mention might be made of a way of viewing the cards without a stereoscope. It sometimes works. Take a piece of card, a postcard say, and hold it sideways on between face and stereo picture, so that one edge of the postcard divides the two images and the other edge touches the vertical line through nose to forehead. Thus each eye can see only one image. Then let the eyes settle down and try to work out the message they are receiving. If unsuccessful, try a longer or a shorter piece of card, since the main problem is finding the correct distance the pictures have to be from the eyes. This method may produce results, but since there may initially be a degree of visual discomfort, and since it is in all probability a dreadfully unhealthy way to treat one's eyes, let it be emphasised that the method is described rather than recommended.

Postcards

The 1850s and 1860s saw the rise of the production of topographical prints for the Victorian scrapbook. Whilst the postcard was still some years in the future, these photographic views laid down the foundations from which the postcard industry was to grow. The best known of the recorders of places was Francis Frith, who began his work in 1860, and whose firm was carried on by his sons after his death in 1898, by which time over 40,000 glass negatives had been accumulated. These views and their successors were to appear in postcard form well into the new century.

In the United States, the sending of cards though the post was permitted in 1867, and picture cards began to appear in the 1870s, but not until late in 1894 did the British authorities allow the posting of pictorial cards. Thus the late Victorian and the Edwardian eras saw a quickly growing traffic of picture postcards, a cheap and efficient means of communication which could arrive later on the same day. Given mankind's apparent instinct to accumulate and retain, it comes as no surprise to learn that our ancestors soon started to collect postcards as well as to send them. The new industry responded to the demand with all manner of pictorial subjects, many of them photographs. The pictures of places are probably of most interest to family historians, unless they can boast one of the much-photographed actors or musical-comedy heroines amongst their forebears. Since a family hoard of postcards is as likely to include places dear to the collector as views sent by holidaying friends, pictures of ancestral background interest may well be inherited. Other cards showing places of family significance can often be found at collectors' fairs and fleamarkets.

The earliest cards were slightly smaller than modern ones, often measuring about 5¼″ × 3¼″ or 4½″ × 3½″ . The latter format was known as court size, and such cards are often identified thus on the back. In November 1899 the 5½″ × 3½″ card was authorised, and this has remained the most popular, though by no means only, size.

Initially, postcards were made by the lithographic process, but from about 1905 photographic cards began to appear on the market, each being individually printed. Though photomechanical reproduction was later introduced, both 'real photograph' and lithographic postcards were still being produced in the 1950s.

It should be pointed out that not all photographs in the postcard format were mass-produced. Portraits, sometimes those taken in studios, but especially those of the more informal kind, were often presented as postcards, complete with divided back and space for stamp. The format enjoyed considerable popularity with seaside promenade photographers between the wars. These examples often have the year and the name of the resort conveniently printed as a border to the photograph. Such individual postcards could be sent through the post, but they often went straight into a photograph album.

It should therefore not be assumed that a postcard portrait can only be of a famous person admired from afar. It may equally well be a relative whose distinction, outside the family circle, may not be for one moment assumed.

Dating Early Photographs

Family historians often need to try to assign a date to pictures they have acquired. Sometimes a date can help us establish which member of a family is pictured. Sometimes the subject's identity is known, but the age can be very difficult to establish, since in old photographs the young can often look very middle-aged and the middle-aged can look old. An idea of the picture's date can help the descendants decide which period of life has been captured.

Various kinds of evidence can be considered in trying to date a photograph: there is the type of photograph, there are aspects of the finished product other than the image, and there is the picture itself. The picture can contain clues in the background and props, in the composition and technique, and in the clothes worn by the sitter. This section deals with some clues which can help in this process of dating. Summaries, in table form for quick reference, are provided later in the book.

It should be pointed out that a period of time rather than a precise year is often the outcome, and an earliest possible date is more likely to be established than a later limit. But if a picture is examined, ideally with a hand magnifying glass, and if all the clues are noted down, a consensus year may emerge, or, more usually, a probable date range may be suggested.

Type of Photograph

Once the type of photograph has been identified, that in itself can give a start to the business of dating, since the date of introduction and the period of popularity of a process are generally known. The details here are, in part, a drawing together of information already touched on, but additional material is also included. Novelties and printing processes are not further discussed at this stage, but are represented on the quick reference chart.

Calotypes and Daguerrotypes

Examples of either of these processes are likely to date from the 1840s. From 1851 onwards they were quickly replaced by the wet collodion process, and both had virtually disappeared by the mid 1850s.

Ambrotypes

Ambrotypes had a fairly short life, corresponding more or less with the third quarter of the nineteenth century. First introduced in the very early 1850s (authorities seem divided between 1851 and 1852), they had largely died out by about 1880. Those in Union Cases are not earlier than 1854, unless they have been re-cased, and the more ornate the decoration on the case, the later it is likely to be.

Cartes de Visite

Cartes were introduced to England in 1858. The 1860s saw their heyday, and their immense popularity had waned a little by the end of the decade, but they continued to be produced in large numbers into the 1890s, and early twentieth century examples can be found. Some photographers were producing unmounted carte-sized pictures as late as the beginning of the Great War.

Cabinet Prints

Though never quite as popular as the 1860s carte, cabinet prints were produced in very large numbers. They were introduced in 1866 and by the 1890s were more common than cartes. They too were still being produced in the early pre-war years of the twentieth century, though the vast majority belong to the Victorian period.

Tintypes

Introduced in about 1856, tintypes quickly became popular and survived, amongst beach and fairground photographers, even as late as 1950. Effectively, tintypes cover the period 1860 to 1940, with most being produced before the First World War.

Stereoscopic Photographs

Stereos, too, had a long life, with their popularity coming in waves. Pre-Great-Exhibition examples are very rare, and the first main wave covered the period from about 1852 to about 1867. By 1856 they were common, and the International Exhibition of 1862 marked a major peak (or, to preserve the image, a crest). Further surges of popularity came in the 1870s and towards the end of the century, but even during the troughs the stereo was by no means dead.

Postcards

British picture postcards are not earlier than September 1894. Size can be of some help in dating the earlier examples, though it is not foolproof. The still common

5½" × 3½" card dates from November 1899. Smaller cards, such as 5¼" × 3¼" or the 4½" × 3½" court card, are likely to date from the second half of the 1890s. The change to the new size in 1899 was not immediate, of course, and postcards have frequently been produced in non-standard sizes. For early postcards, however, dating deductions based on measurements may be made with a fair degree of probability.

Roll Film Prints

In theory, size can help in dating pictures printed from roll film negatives. In practice, the position is complicated by a number of factors: new negative sizes were constantly being introduced; old sizes were given a new lease of life by being used in new cameras; cameras were devised which recorded two photographs on the same length of film that other cameras used for one. There is the further fact that the image size of the picture that survives may not be that of the original negative, since it may have been enlarged. As the edges of the image may have been lost in the enlarging, the measurements of the resulting print may not even be in proportion to those of the original negative. Thus, though precise information can be given about the introduction of new formats, image size proves to be of dubious value in dating, and this should be borne in mind when trying to make use of the details which follow.

Eastman's earliest roll film negatives were circular, with a 2½" diameter, and appeared in 1888. Round pictures of this size, at least, can be pinned down to a period. In the same year a rival company brought out the Stirn 'America' camera, which gave 3" × 4" pictures. Without the supporting processing service that Eastman offered, however, the 'America' made much less impact. In 1895 the Pocket Kodak produced pictures which were 2" × 1". But it was with the Brownie cameras that popular photography really took off. The first of the series, launched in 1900, gave 2¼" square images, and the Number 2 Brownie, dating from 1901 or 1902 (sources are either contradictory or vague), introduced the 2¼" × 3¼" snapshot. This size was to prove enormously popular, and it survived for over half a century.

Another popular size, introduced in 1912, was 2½" × 1⅝", as given by 127 film in the Kodak Vest Pocket camera. This camera remained in production until the mid 1920s, but the film survived much longer, particularly for use in the Brownie 127, a bakelite camera which became a very common choice for first-time buyers.

So far the concern has been with box cameras, but roll film folding cameras also appeared in the late 1890s, and enjoyed some favour in the years before the First World War. Generally, folding cameras could give larger negatives than their box relations, and one early model took full-plate pictures, 8½" × 6½". Such a size meant too cumbersome a camera for easy use, and quarter plate (3¼″ × 4¼″) and postcard (3¼″ × 5½″) were more common picture sizes for roll film folding cameras in the first fifteen years of the twentieth century.

It was, though, not until the 1930s that the folding camera really came into its own, so examples of roll film photographs tend more often to date from this later period.

If the 1930s saw a boom in larger roll film pictures, they also saw an increase in small negatives. The Box Tengor gave sixteen pictures, 2¼″ × 1¼″, from films which had previously produced eight snaps, and the Baby Tengor used 127 film, but gave pictures which measured 1¼″ × 1½″. Small negatives were, of course, a more reasonable proposition once enlargement was more widely practised.

If generalisation is possible, and it is made with some reluctance, the position may be summed up thus:

1. Very few roll film pictures are earlier than 1900, and most are Edwardian or later.
2. Negatives measuring 2½″ × 1⅝″ are not earlier than 1912.
3. The larger sizes tend to date from after (often well after) the Great War, but postcard and quarter plate pictures could come from the years immediately before it.
4. Particular measurements could point to the use of a camera of known date, but could also mislead.

Evidence other than the Image

The backs of photographs and the card on which cartes and cabinets are mounted can also give some pointers towards dating.

There is always the chance of some handwritten evidence identifying the sitter and giving age or date. Such gifts of information are disappointingly rare, and their rareness should, of course, encourage us to document our own photographs better than we often do, for our ancestors are not alone in failing to provide for the curiosity of later generations. Another possible piece of handwritten evidence is a photographer's reference number. This tied in with their own records and could enable them to find a negative if a reprint should be required. If a firm or its successor has survived, there is just the possibility that its order books have survived too. The odds must be against such good fortune, but it could be a way of ascertaining a date, and perhaps an address as well.

Printed evidence, too, which may be copious on the back of cartes and cabinets, can offer clues. The name and address of the photographer may be significant, and this will be discussed in the next section. But there may also be dates. Occasionally the card bears a printed date, which, of course, refers to the printing of the batch of mounts rather than the image itself. Unless the photographer did much worse business than expected, however, such a date is not likely to be very much older than the photograph. Dates of the "not earlier than …" variety are more usual. In this category can be found the year in which a firm was established, though the longer this was before the date of the actual photograph, the more impressive and valuable would be its publicity value. Few firms boast of an establishment date until it conveys a sense of respectability and durability. Dates of exhibitions, medals and prizes are also common. A clue to dating might also sometimes be found in the mention of distinguished patrons. "Photographers to Her Majesty the Queen and Their Royal Highnesses the Prince and Princess of Wales" merely places a picture between 1863 and 1901, but research might lead to something more precise with "Photographers to His Highness Akbaloddowla, ex-King of Oude", depending on how early that king's retirement proved to be.

Some backs tell of electrically lit studios. Since electric lighting was widely introduced in the 1880s, and since there would be little point, in later years, in bragging about something that had become commonplace, such pictures are most likely to belong to that decade.

The overall design of the back of cartes and cabinets can also be informative. In the 1860s designs tended to be simple, often just a small trade plate on a large white background. Information was often limited to the name and address of the photographer. In the 1870s designs became more ornate and often grew to fill the whole space available. Elaboration reached its height in the 1880s, when the cards were often packed with information, giving addresses of other branches and listing medals, exhibitions and famous patrons. Lettering could be elaborate, and coloured mounts began to be used. By the 1890s a self-conscious artistic quality was often found. Dark coloured card became widespread, with white or, more opulent, gold printing. Information was still copious, but there were often pictures as well: artists' easels, coats of arms, ferns, pheasants, flowers and, especially, cherubs. In tribute to the artistic endeavours of those whose work they promote, the cherubs are often busy little chaps, sketching earnestly, or taking pictures of ladies who seem in no way discomposed at being confronted by a photographer wearing nothing but bird or butterfly wings.

Sometimes details can be taken in conjunction. "Established in 1885" and a reference to the Queen as patron gives a period of 16 years, of which the latter half is more likely in view of what has been said about the use of establishment dates. Sometimes different pictures from the same studio can each contribute towards dating. The Parisian School of Photography (at Fleet Street and Old Kent Road) boasts "Established 1851" on one photograph and "Established over 25 years" on another. This suggests the late 1880s as the date for the second photograph. (If much later, why not "Established over 30 years"?)

Even the corners of a carte or cabinet can help. In the 1860s they were normally square cut, but later they were generally rounded. Caution is necessary, however, since there was some re-emergence of squared corners in the 1880s.

Before moving on to other types of picture, one other detail might be mentioned. On the back of photographs from the United States a postage stamp, used to indicate the payment of tax, indicates that the picture dates from the period 1st September 1864 to 1st August 1866.

With stereos, too, some help can be given by the card itself. Very early examples, dating from the 1850s, may be mounted on very thin card. From the end of the 1850s the publisher's name may appear on the margin surrounding the actual pictures. The lack of a publisher's name does not indicate an early card, but the presence of a name does suggest about 1858 or later. Towards the end of the 1860s publicity information began to appear on the back of the card, though again, a blank back does not necessarily point to an earlier period. Corners were generally square until the end of the 1880s, and often rounded thereafter.

The colour of the card may also be relevant, though this is not enormously reliable. There was some taste in the 1850s for mounting stereo pictures on pale grey card, and some use of yellow card in the 1860s. Other colours enjoyed some favour from the 1870s. But colour is not as useful a guide as it is with cartes and cabinets.

The backs of postcards can also prove informative. The divided back was not authorised until 1902 in Britain. Before that date the whole of one side had to be given over to the address, with picture or message (or both) restricted to the front. Inevitably it took a while for old stocks to be sold off and for the change to be completed, so it is perhaps safer to assume that the switch from undivided backs took a year or so. Once the back had been divided, it was common for "Communication" to be printed at the top of the left hand section and "Address" at the top to the right. On earlier divided examples, when the revised regulations were still something of a novelty, a fuller explanation often appeared on the left, such as, "For Inland Postage ONLY, this space may now be used for communications". The presence of such directions may suggest a date in the years immediately following the change, though allowance should again be made for old stock taking some time to sell out before new cards with a simpler heading were printed. In practice, cards as late as 1905 can be found with "now" still included in the wording, and cards as early as 1904 can be found where the "now" has been dropped. By 1907 it was possible for the back to be shared between message and address on some overseas postcards as well as those to inland destinations, and instructions either became more complicated, specifying additional parts of the world, or simpler, with mention of permissible destinations being omitted entirely.

If a card was posted, the postmark, if legible, will give a precise date for the event, though the image may well have been made at an earlier date. Some scenes continued to be reproduced for many years. One view by Roger Fenton, who died in 1869, was still in postcard use as late as 1970. The chances, however, of someone sending a seriously out-of-date portrait must, except in cases of marked vanity, be fairly slim.

If the postmark cannot be made out, at least the monarch, Victoria, or, far more probably, Edward VII or George V, will give some indication of date: 1901 or earlier, 1901 to 1910, and 1910 or later, respectively. But the value of the stamp can also be revealing. Before 3rd June 1918 the inland postal rate for postcards was ½d. From June 3rd 1918 to 12th June 1921 it was 1d. From 13th June 1921 to 23rd May 1922 the price rose to 1½d, but then dropped again, on 24th May 1922, to 1d. Monarch and value, taken together, can sometimes narrow the time-scale quite usefully. Thus, a George V ½d stamp dates a postcard to the period 1910 to 1918. After June 1918, incidentally, increased prices of both postage and product brought about a reduction in the popularity of postcard communication.

Even if the card was not sent by post, and many portraits in postcard format were never intended to be, it was usual for a space for a stamp to be indicated on the top right-hand corner of the back. In this space, at least during the ½d post period, the value of the required stamp was often printed.

One final piece of information from the back of cards can be the words "court post card", which, as indicated during the discussion of sizes, point to the period from 1894 to 1899.

Names and Addresses of Photographers

The name of the photographic firm and the details of its premises, as found on the back of photographs, can be used in conjunction with trade directories to assist the business of dating.

Photographers, naturally enough, appeared in trade directories, which would be brought out for a town or county at, say, 3–4 year intervals. In a series of directories a firm's changes of name, mergers and moves of premises can be traced. The information on the back of photographs, cartes and cabinet prints especially, can then be tied in with the list of directory entries, to see with which point in time the firm's title and studio(s), as given on the reverse of the picture, coincide.

Two words of caution are necessary. The information in a directory will have been collected over a period of months before publication and may already be incorrect when it appears. A photographer might well use up an existing stock of cards for mounting before going to the expense of having new cards printed.

Either directory or picture could thus bear information that had already, if fairly recently, become out-of-date. The conclusion must therefore be that time bands based on photograph/directory comparisons should be treated as approximate at either extreme.

In undertaking such comparisons, the family historian will usually have a fair amount of investigation to do before any kind of conclusion can be reached, but some lists of photographers' directory entries have been compiled. David Cory's valuable work on Norwich photographers, mentioned in the bibliography, has been drawn on in the following two examples, and has made the task much easier.

Picture A shows, in vignette, the head and shoulders of a woman in her thirties, who is wearing a high-collared dress of watered silk. The back tells us that the photographer was Shrubsole of Norwich, with premises at Exchange Street Corner and Davey Place. From directories it appears that William Lewis Shrubsole opened his first studio at Ely Place in 1879. By 1888 he had four studios, including the two already mentioned, but by 1892 only Exchange Street Corner and Davey Place remained. In 1894 both of these studios had gone, and there was a new studio at Briggs Street. This suggests that the portrait was taken some time after 1888 and before 1894, with 1892 as the one known date when just the right combination of studios existed.

Picture B is of a frock-coated gent of late middle or vigorous old age. It was taken by J.R.Sawyer at Sawyer's Italian Studio, 46 London Street, Norwich. J.R. Sawyer was operating at 42 London Street until about 1864, when he moved to number 46. In about 1873 a new partner joined the firm, which was thenceforth known as Sawyer and Bird, and a renumbering of houses gave the premises a new address, number 32, in about 1875. Thus the picture appears to date from the approximate period 1864–1873. The sitter is shown at full length in a chair, before a drape and a backcloth depicting classical architecture, and beside a classical looking plinth, which suggests, as will shortly be shown, that the carte may belong to the sixties rather than the seventies.

No mention has yet been made of the family historian's tried and moderately trusted friend, the census. Certainly photographers named on photographs may be linked with their census addresses, but censuses are a full ten years apart and are likely to name the practitioner rather than the firm, and to give a home address which may or may not have been used for business. On its own, therefore, the census is likely to be of very limited use, whereas a directory gives a commercial identification in a form just like that used on the pictures themselves. At best, a census may provide supporting evidence when taken in conjunction with information given by trade directories.

The Image – Studio Background and Props

The studio settings in which sitters were placed can be a source of much pleasure and entertainment. Young ladies sit, in their indoor best, in leafy glades and before turbulent seas. Children stare insecurely out from seats of swings set at a frozen tilt. Babies sag in voluminous furs, half propped up by parental hands sticking out from between the folds. Clerical gentlemen try to look erudite in studies full of painted-on book spines. A young man grips the back of a chair conveniently found by a lakeside. A family poses against a background of outdoor classical architecture which is half hidden by an incongruous indoor curtain.

As well as affording innnocent amusement, the backcloths, furniture and props of the Victorian photographer's studio can offer hints as to the date of a picture. Of course, settings can only provide a rough guide, since, especially in the provinces, a photographer might hang on to his props and furnishings for years, shuffling them about in new combinations. Nevertheless, considered in conjunction with other kinds of information, the studio trappings can suggest further time bands which can be compared to those indicated by other evidence, for props and backgrounds had their own fashions and periods of popularity.

In the 1860s (and in the late 1850s as far as cartes are concerned) settings were generally relatively simple. Some subjects stand or sit against neutral backgrounds, with or without a curtain hanging down at one side. If the subject is seated, he or she may be at a small table or writing desk, and may be holding a book. The taste for drapery, seen in curtains, may extend to a table covering as well. Also favoured in the middle of the decade was the classical look. Columns, arches, plinths and balustrades abound, often supplemented by the ubiquitous length of curtain. As the sixties drew to a close, chairs remained a popular prop, but were often present for leaning on with one hand, rather than for sitting purposes. Also at the end of the decade came a taste for painted windows looking out on a painted country scene. This fashion faded away in the 1870s when, instead of offering glimpses of a supposed rural world, the photographer's studio often pretended to move out into the open air.

The 1870s were the age of the rustic background. Large backdrops of natural settings were used, and props were provided to match. We see stiles, rock gardens, bridges, fences and landscaped steps set against masses of painted foliage. Any studio might offer the background of a woodland pool; the more ambitious might add a cardboard swan. Seaside backgrounds can also be found, and there is some attempt to cater for children with, still on a maritime theme, ships' masts and rigging for boys. Girls might have to content themselves with a stereotypical basket of flowers.

The chair was still popular, and could be introduced into improbable outdoor contexts. By the latter part of the 1870s, chairs were increasingly elaborate with padded backs, in line with their common function of being leaned against instead of sat on. Padded rests and lecterns served the same purpose and, like the chairs, continued into the new decade.

The eighties offer not so much that is different but often the recipe as before, though made up to a richer mixture. Artificial rocks and tussocks strew the ground, and swings and hammocks may be found suspended from conveniently unseen branches. The balustrade, sometimes more weathered or mossy than before, makes a comeback. And indoors, for indoor settings had not become extinct, an oriental flavour may be added by a Chinese or Japanese screen. Occasionally a wholly new setting, such as a railway carriage, may be found.

In the 1890s the taste for a touch of the exotic, already shown by oriental screens, might find expression in pot plants, palm trees and even cockatoos. The desire for a sense of modernity might be satisfied by the inclusion of a bicycle. Babies snuggle in rugs of white fur and adults pose by mirrors. There can be a highly contrived air about garden sets, with art triumphing firmly over nature. One way and another, there can be a sense that the designer-photographer is trying hard.

Yet contrivance is not the most obvious feature of pictures from the nineties, since a significant fashion in composition was for a close-up of the sitter, with little or no background in evidence. Studio backgrounds, when seen, might be wilfully fanciful, but concentration on the face, as described in the next section, was much more characteristic of the decade.

The Image – Composition and Technique

Even the way in which the photographer dealt with the subject can reflect the changing fashions. Whilst it may be considered only a rough guide, the closer the camera is to the sitter, the later the photograph was taken.

In the late 1850s and in the 1860s the full-length figure is most common. The figure may be standing or sitting, perhaps with a book in hand, but in either case the feet are likely to be included in the picture. Seated figures are most often found on relatively early cartes and cabinet prints. The use of a chair or chairs to give tightness and variety of height to a small group was, and of course remains, a natural strategy, and so pictures of two or more people are less datable in this way. But single full-length sitting figures certainly belong more often to the fifties and early sixties than to later years. As the 1860s progressed, the full-length standing figure using a chair or balustrade as a hand rest became a popular image.

In the 1870s and 1880s the camera tends to move closer. Figures are presented in three-quarter length, with the bottom of the picture cutting across a line somewhere between shins and mid-thigh. A chair (by now, often, the top part of a chair) or a lectern-like rest is still there to hold on to, especially in the 1870s. Seated figures are less common, and their feet, too, are likely to be out of the picture.

As the 1880s moved into the 1890s, the camera came in further still, and the last decade of the century was very much the age of head and shoulders portraits. This closing-in was frequently further emphasised by the practice of vignetting, whereby the outer parts of the picture are white, and head and shoulders appear in an oval exposed area in the centre. The oval (or roundish) shape is sometimes very distinct. Sometimes, because the background is pale anyway, the fading away of the image into whiteness is most evident around the shoulder line, with the head standing out strongly against the all-white background of the upper part of the picture. The huge popularity of the vignette can be a little depressing to the modern eye, because it cuts out details of clothing and studio setting, but the technique is highly characteristic of its time and points very firmly towards the later years of the century.

The Image – Exterior Background

In outdoor photographs there is also, at least in theory, some chance of dating the scene from its details. In practice, helpful details may prove elusive. In countryside scenes there is precious little to date. Flora and fauna can become extinct or be introduced, but they are not in the habit of presenting themselves for inspection in family photographs. In townscapes, buildings are of little help, unless they are both identifiable and demonstrably very new, or, better still, just being built. In streetscapes, the arrival on the scene of certain inventions might be thought to offer an earliest possible date. Unfortunately, however, most such inventions saw the light of day in Victorian times. Though there were, of course, professionals taking outdoor pictures before the advent of roll film, the vast majority of family photographs set in the open air are from roll-film cameras, and, indeed, from those popular models which date from early Edwardian rather than late Victorian times. The potentially useful inventions, therefore, tend to predate the age of outdoor snaps, and the fact that the picture was taken in the open air suggests a later date than the earliest possible year indicated by the inventions themselves. When Victoria died, trains were long established, telephones (and, hence, telegraph poles) had arrived, and street lighting was already starting on the transition from gas to electricity. Pneumatic-tyred bicycles, with a fairly modern look, had been around since the 1880s, electric trams had started to appear on the streets in the 1890s, and in the last years of the century the motor car had made its début, with the Prince of Wales taking his first ride in 1898. Whilst the real growth in the number of cars did not come until the ten years preceding the First War, the presence of a car in a picture is no guarantee of an Edwardian date. Even manned flight had made a modest beginning, with Sir Hiram Maxim's Flying Machine travelling through the air for a distance of some three hundred feet in 1894. It was not until the first ten years of the new century that the motor-powered bus started to spread, but generally those inventions that the unpractised eye might readily identify are older than the kinds of photograph most likely to record them, and they are therefore not very helpful in dating.

Naturally, expertise could help further. A researcher well-versed in the detailed history of transport and able to recognise specific models of car, bus or tram, a student familiar with the evolution of street lighting and furniture, or a devotee of early twentieth century agricultural machinery could all achieve some success in dating outdoor pictures. This work can pretend to no such kinds of expertise.

There do remain, however, some chances to glean clues. Shop signs, if the area can be identified, may be checked against trade directories, which offer a useful record of the changing population of streets housing traders and other businesses.

It should also be remembered that special events bring out the photographer in us all. Queen Victoria's Diamond Jubilee, for instance, coinciding as it did with the early years of roll film, if not with the massive boom in its use just after her death, produced a land full of decorations, processions and celebrations asking to be recorded. If a special event seems to be the subject of a picture, and if the locality is known, it should be possible to obtain useful advice on the nature and date of the event from archivists, libraries, local history societies or newspaper records.

A case history illustrates the point well. A collection of roll-film negatives, bought at a King's Lynn market, included several photographs of a flooded town. When printed up, the pictures showed flooded streets, an interested crowd and stranded cars at the far end of a watery vista, a horse and cart splashing past shoe and pie shops, and a boy paddling along with his boots hung by the laces around his neck. Above the boy, on the wall of a building behind him, was a road name, "Cowgate Street". Given the Norfolk origin of the find, it seemed reasonable to start by considering Norfolk towns, and particularly towns large enough to have been walled in the past. Since King's Lynn itself had several gates, but no Cowgate, the next obvious contender was Norwich. A look at a modern map was enough to establish that the city still has a street called Cowgate. After that, it simply took a trip to the record office, where expert help quickly produced the information that Norwich had been flooded in 1912. The Cowgate area had been affected and the archivist was able to add that Reeves' Pie Shop, past which the horse was wading in another picture, had been in nearby Magdalen Street.

Though this story is a pleasant example of success, it has to be admitted that dating outdoor photographs from their background may often have more to do with serendipity than with system.

The Image – Costume

Clothing is a very good pointer to a photograph's approximate date. The more conversant one is with the history of costume, the more clues one can find in a picture. The topic is a large one, and one where the average inspector of family photographs may be inclined to stop short of thoroughgoing expertise. But even the untutored eye can accustom itself to picking out some useful information, and it is to the moderately willing, if untrained, eye that this section attempts to offer assistance.

As ever, there are warning notes to be sounded. People tended to wear their Sunday best to the photographer's studio, and that best may have been required to last for a good few years. So clothes may not be entirely up-to-the-minute. Generally, the older the sitter, the more likely he or she is to be out of fashion. It is also the case that there could be a time lag between London and the provinces, so that sitters outside the capital, as well as sitters who were less well off, might not take up new fashions for a year or few. This delay could sometimes be offset by the fact that at least some photographers had sets of clothes available for hire, but it remains true that fashion details tend to give an earliest rather than a latest possible date.

Men's clothes in particular can be difficult to date. Some of the changes they underwent were less dramatic than those of women's clothes, and men, especially once they reached middle age, were less likely to keep up with fashion. Perhaps more to the point, though, is that details can be harder to distinguish on men's often uniformly dark clothing. One field of male costume which may be uncharacteristically datable is military uniform. This, however, is rather a specialist field, where the regiment has to be identified before progress can be made, and where background research may need to be extensive and supported by informed advice.

If all this seems discouraging, it should be re-emphasised that details of costume can, in spite of problems, give the lay viewer very significant aid. Whilst the majority of photographs to survive date from the 1860s and later, some attention is given here to clothes of the preceding years as well, since some family historians are lucky enough to have earlier pictures in their collection.

Women

By starting with a consideration of general line and impression, we fall immediately into generalisation. Nevertheless, some idea of the broad trends gives a useful starting point before particular aspects of clothing are dwelt on.

In the 1840s women wore fairly close-fitting garments on the top half of their bodies, whilst skirts were fairly full, giving a smooth bell-shape. In the fifties and sixties the contrast between the close-fitting bodice and the full skirt became far more marked, for this was the age of the crinoline. The 1870s saw the first period of the bustle, which sloped away into a full, uncrinolined skirt. This was generally a decade of complicated designs, and a very popular look in the early 1870s was the 'Dolly Varden' dress, where the bodice was connected to a short, bunched-up overskirt, with a full, loose skirt below. In the first half of the eighties the Princess line came into vogue, with its tight, long waist brought to a point in front. The eighties also marked the second period of the bustle, though this time it was worn high, jutting out from the small of the back. In the latter half of the eighties the tailored suit with blouse made its appearance, and this went on to prove even more popular in the nineties. Corsetry was often tight through both eighties and nineties. By the nineties, however, the fashion emphasis had switched. If the earlier decades had stressed the skirt, with crinoline or bustle, the nineties paid more attention to the top half of the body, with a highlighting of arms and shoulders. Skirts became relatively plain. The new century ushered in a sleeker look both above and below. Corsetry created a heavy busted, S-shaped stance for the first few years of the century, and blouse and skirt combinations became very popular. From about 1908, however, the S-shape became less marked, and in 1909 a close-fitting tube of a dress came in, with a long hobble skirt, narrowed at the ankles.

All of this is, of course, very general, and when particular garments are considered, some more detail can be added to the picture.

In the earliest photographs, clothes appear to fit the upper body and arms fairly closely, and in the period of the crinoline, from about 1850 to about 1865, the bodice was noticeably cut to hug the figure. As the fifties gave way to the sixties, there was a fashion for epaulettes on the shoulders, marked with braid trimming, and these continued to enjoy some favour until the early 1870s. Sleeves in the 1860s were generally wide, long and set in low on the shoulder. The upper part was sometimes puffed, and the general effect, especially in the first half of the decade, was of a markedly sloping look to the shoulder line. In the late sixties and early seventies a square yoked effect to the bodice was popular, and this might be defined by braid or fringing.A fashion which followed in the mid-seventies was the Cuirasse bodice, with a front panel and a military air. During the seventies the overall shape of the bodice remained simple, and sleeves were set in high on the shoulder, so that the sloping look disappeared from about 1870. In the 1880s bodices tended to be closely figure-fitting and buttoned up to the throat, whilst the nineties saw a variety of blouses, jackets, short boleros and dress bodices cut to look like jackets. All were popular, and all could be distinctly elaborate. At the very end of the eighties things started to happen to sleeves. At first there was the narrow sleeve, brought to a peak at the shoulder. The peak grew fuller and more rounded until, in the mid-nineties, it had taken on the puffed-out appearance of shoulder or upper arm that is well-known as the leg-of-mutton style. There was also some vogue in the middle years of the nineties for a rather different kind of sleeve which was three-quarter length and which ended in a frill. Towards the end of the century the leg-of-mutton look disappeared rather abruptly and sleeves became close-fitting all the way down. Their tightness in the first years of the twentieth century might be relieved by a little fullness or puffing at the shoulder, but they no longer ballooned out, and they were often long, sometimes covering half the hand. Blouses and bolero jackets, both favoured in the nineties, became, if anything, more popular in the early twentieth century, and they were often highly elaborate. Until about 1908 the blouse might be allowed to hang over at the waist, but this floppiness of silhouette disappeared thereafter.

Below the waist, too, fashion came and went. The smooth, bell-shaped skirt of the 1840s became increasingly full. For the first half of the 1850s it was filled out by multiple layers of petticoat, but 1856 saw the introduction of the cage crinoline, a hooped petticoat held out by whalebone or watchspring. By 1860 the cage crinoline was at its widest, sitting was a major undertaking, and two women could not occupy the same sofa. In the second half of the sixties the fullness of skirts began to recede; many women abandoned crinolines altogether, and the half crinoline (the back half) made a brief appearance at the very end of the decade. The general tendency when the crinoline disappeared, was for skirts to be flatter at the front but full at the back. This fullness turned, in the late sixties and first half of the seventies, into the bustle, where the folds of flowing material were caught up into a bunch behind. This bundle of swathed material fell away in a sloping line at the back of the skirt. One lady, asked how she achieved such an effective bustle, confided that she padded it out with newspaper, and that she found 'The Times' particularly suited to the purpose. Frills, ribbons, buttons and fringing were all called upon, in the first half of the seventies, to aid the general splendour of the effect. Skirts remained flat-fronted through these years and into the eighties, but in the latter half of the seventies the bunched-up bustle lapsed from favour, though the garments remained full at the back, often falling into a train. In the first half of the eighties the bustle made a return, though with a changed silhouette: instead of sloping away it was higher and larger, sticking out horizontally from the small of the back before falling away sharply towards the ground. The overskirt disappeared by about 1894, and the nineties and the first decade of the twentieth century saw simpler skirts, tight at the waist, smooth over the hips, and flaring out, bell-shaped, below. Gores and trains often gave body to the garments. In the few years preceding the Great War drapery tended to fall more softly, and there emerged an emphasis on narrowness of the hips. In 1909 the hobble skirt made its début. This long skirt, narrowed at the ankles, created a line not dissimilar to that of men's peg-top trousers (of which something in due course).

Whilst skirts and bodices account for the main features of a particular look, there remain other details to consider. The head and neck were also subject to the dictates of fashion. At the end of the 1840s hair worn in dangling side ringlets, with a bun at the back, was common. In fashion too, though also found both earlier and later, was the bonnet with a full, forward-pointing brim, and with ties under the chin. In the fifties relatively plain hairstyles were favoured, with the hair smoothed back into a simple bun from a central parting. For day dresses, necklines were high, with a small collar and, perhaps, a brooch. The once universal, small, white indoor caps had, by about 1855, been largely discarded by the younger women, especially those who were unmarried, in favour of ribbons or hairnets. Simplicity of hairstyles was often preserved into the 1860s, though the visibility of ears can provide additional information. Hair tended to cover the ears in the earlier part of the decade, whereas ears were more likely to be exposed from the middle to late sixties. Not all styles of the sixties were simple, though, for the chignon style became common, with the hair massed over a pad at the back of the head. In the second half of the sixties a pork-pie style of hat had some currency, worn square on the head. The 1870s were very much the age of the elaborate coiffure, particularly in the earlier years, with ornate styles built up on artificial hair, and with the back of the head echoing the shape of the back of the skirt. One firm at the time was said to be turning out two tons of artificial hair a week. In the second half of the decade the exuberance died down somewhat, and the bun made a reappearance, now often worn high on the head. In the seventies, too, Princess Alexandra adopted the fringe, which she was to wear for the rest of her life, and she was much copied. Necklines of the seventies were varied, with use frequently made of scarves and jabots. In the eighties hair and necklines calmed down. Small standing collars became popular, buttoned to the throat and perhaps set off with a piecrust frill. Hair tended to be more simply dressed, following the outline of the head in smooth contours, with the bun, if worn, at the back rather than on top. The fringe survived on many heads, frequently, especially in the early eighties, with a crimped, straggly or tousled look. But if hair and collars took on a degree of sobriety, all of the imagination went into the hats, which could be trimmed not just with fur and feathers but with the original owners of the fur and feathers. Whole dead creatures, birds, their nests, small rodents and even large insects were all called on to decorate outdoor headgear.

Indoors, the white caps were, by the later eighties, worn only by old women; the younger married women had followed the unmarried in dispensing with their use. Elaborate hats reminiscent of a natural history museum survived into the nineties, though any one hat might carry a smaller and more modest range of wildlife decoration than in earlier years. Smaller hats, firmly centred on the head, were often worn, though still often sporting at least a feather or two. The straw hat or boater also enjoyed the favour of women as well as men. Necklines became very high for day dresses, with stand-up collars, and with the piecrust frill still much in evidence. The bun was still widespread in the nineties, but fringes had become rare, and the last few years of the century saw the door-knocker or teapot-handle style, with hair looped or coiled at the back of the head. The opening years of the new century brought in hair dressed high on the head, and from about 1910 the enormous, wide-brimmed hat was much in vogue.

Finally a word might be said about general trimmings, pattern and colour. The 1860s, especially the first half, were often marked by a taste for geometrical patterns on skirts and sleeves. In the 1870s dresses were often loaded down with trimmings. Significant improvements had been made in sewing machines in the late fifties and in the sixties, and these bore fruit in the fancy stitching, frills, ornamental buttons and fringing of women's clothes. New dyes led to brighter colours, though these are not likely to be evident in monochrome photographs, and a mixture of colours and materials in the same dress was common, sometimes creating an effect suggestive of patchwork. The eighties saw an inclination towards plainer, more severe effects, though the contrasting tendency to disguise the top of the head, especially, as part of South Kensington has already been noticed. The nineties, were marked by a growing taste for the use of lace, especially on blouses, and by the craze for jet ornaments. The love of lace continued through Edwardian times, and feather boas were also popular at this period.

It is, perhaps, a pity that so much invention and industry should now present itself to our eyes in muted black (or sepia) and white.

Men

To move to the consideration of men's fashions is to enter a simpler and rather more sober world, with less frequent changes. This was not necessarily because the male did not take trouble with his appearance, but rather, perhaps, because he was busy projecting a different kind of self-image on the world.

As with women, the overall look provides the starting point. In the forties and on into the fifties suits were tight and fitted close to the body. Towards the end of the fifties they became looser fitting, with wider sleeves and legs. It was not considered necessary for the top and bottom halves of the ensemble to match, and until the mid-sixties a dark jacket worn with light trousers was common. By the second half of the sixties the lounge suit had achieved a degree of popularity and was often characterised by deep cuffs. In the seventies suits became tighter again, even though the jackets were often double-breasted. A rather straight, narrow line to male costume persisted through much of the eighties until, at the end of the decade, a baggier look to suits came in and lasted to the end of the century. Lounge suits, introduced a good while earlier, were very widespread indeed in the 1890s, and from about 1900 they were the normal day wear.

Some of what can be said about jackets has been said in the course of considering the ensemble, but a few more details of upper-body garments may be added. In the 1840s waistcoats often bore fancy patterns, and not until the mid-seventies was it customary that they should match the jacket. From the late fifties jackets were generally fastened by just the top button. Particular styles appeared, or had their moment of glory, at particular times. The short, double-breasted 'reefer' jacket found some favour in the 1860s, especially amongst men of the lower-middle and labouring classes. Interestingly, encouraged perhaps by some taste for shorter jackets amongst young men in the late seventies, the reefer jacket was often chosen in the first half of the eighties, and a little beyond, to convey a sporting look. This may be a fairly unusual example of a fashion becoming upwardly mobile. Norfolk jackets, with a belt and vertical pleats, came in during the second half of the 1870s and grew considerably in popularity in the eighties and after. From about 1894 the Norfolk jacket often had a yoke set into it – a feature not normally found earlier. The blazer, worn as a sports jacket, dates from the late seventies, and 1888 saw the arrival of the dinner jacket (known, though, as the dress lounge jacket until 1896). One final piece of torso-wear, the cummerbund, became popular with formal dress in the 1890s.

Some details of trousers can also help with dating. In the fifties and early sixties the peg-top trouser was in vogue. Wide-legged, but tapering to a close fit at the ankles, these garments were often striped or checked. In the late fifties and through the sixties a raised or braided side seam was fashionable, and such emphasis on seams became a standard feature of evening dress trousers from the 1870s. Knickerbockers, loosely cut and gathered into a band below the knee, made their first appearance in the 1860s but are of little real use for dating, since they enjoyed a long life on into the twentieth century. The first half of the nineties saw a brief comeback for the peg-top trouser, though more usually in plain material for this reincarnation. During the same half decade turn-ups featured in the wardrobe of the more dashing young men, though it was not until shortly before the First World War that they became a standard feature of trousers. In the mid-nineties the trouser-press was introduced, and creases were subsequently often in evidence.

Turning to the extremities, feet in the forties and fifties were often encased in square-toed shoes. In the seventies and eighties toes were relatively pointed. Spats can be found from the 1870s onward.

Further up the body, high coat and shirt collars mark the early years of photographed history, with the large, loose cravat being favoured through the forties and fifties. Ties of a rather narrower kind gained ground from the mid-sixties. The end of the century saw high shirt collars return with a vengeance, with a maximum height of some three inches being reached by 1899. The high collar continued into the new century.

Last comes the hat. The top hat was worn throughout Victorian times, though by the end of the century it had taken on the formality with which it has ever since been associated. There were, however, some changes in design. In the forties and fifties the crown tended to be very high, and pictures of men in stove-pipe hats generally date from the early photographic period. If the medium-height crown is then taken as the norm, two periods of relatively low crowns can be discerned – the sixties and the nineties. The lower crowns were quite common in these decades, but by no means universal. Top hat brims also underwent change. Before about 1865 the brim was flattish. There may have been some curling of the sides, but the line where brim joined crown was straight. From the mid-sixties a noticeably curved line of brim was often apparent. In the seventies, especially in the second half, top hat brims were often, though not always, rather narrow. The bowler of the sixties often appeared low-crowned, narrow-brimmed and rather flat-topped, with an outline something like that of a pudding basin. In the seventies a rather high-crowned bowler was common. In the eighties and nineties the bowlers were medium-crowned with curled brim and had a generally modern look. The homburg first became popular in the mid-1870s and the straw boater came in at much the same time, though not until the nineties did it enjoy its golden age.

Children

A systematic account of children's clothing would give limited aid in dating, often indicating the age of the child rather than the age of the photograph. (The older the child, the longer the skirt or trousers.) Sometimes children's clothes echoed those of adults. Girls, like women, wore crinolines for instance, though theirs were shorter, revealing ankle-length pantaloons, and their bodices were often low-necked and short-sleeved, proving more like the evening wear than the day wear of their elders. There were, however, some aspects of children's fashions which can help towards dating, even though the long life of certain looks means that this help can be rather vague.

Full length trousers on young boys are generally a pointer to the forties or very early fifties. After that, trouser length related to age. For both sexes a Scottish flavour was popular during the sixties and seventies and expressed itself in plaids, sporrans and tartan dresses. The taste for dressing sisters alike, except for the age-related skirt length, was perhaps strongest in the sixties and seventies, though it is a taste that seems never wholly to have died out. About half way through the sixties sailor suits for boys began to put in an appearance, and this nautical look became increasingly popular through the seventies. By the eighties girls' versions appeared, with a skirt complementing the sailor top, and the fashion survived through the rest of the century and beyond. The seventies produced dresses for girls as elaborate as those of their elders. In the eighties smocked yokes came in as something of a novelty, which went on in later years to become almost de rigueur. The eighties, too, produced a new look in boys' clothing, when parents (though not necessarily sons) went overboard for the Little Lord Fauntleroy suit, with its velvet trousers and jacket and its broad, frilled collar. Late in the eighties lace-up shoes for children became an alternative to the previously standard buttoned boots. In the nineties a sombreness of colour crept into clothes for both sexes, with styles firmly echoing those of adults.

Before leaving children's clothes, one point should be made which has to do with identification of subject rather than dating of picture. With children of pre-school age, skirts and long hair are no guide to sex, for both boys and girls were dressed in the same way through Victorian and Edwardian times. The sweet little girl on Great-Grandmother's lap may very well be Grandfather.

Other Photographic Items

As well as photographs themselves, other photographic items may have been passed down to the researcher. Their market value may be low, but their value as ancestral objects and as attractive artefacts may be considerable. Whilst any lengthy discussion of such items is beyond the scope of this work, some passing mention of the most common may be pardoned.

Cameras

Whilst an earlier heirloom is possible, camera-owning became a reality for the population at large in the late 1880s and the 1890s with the proliferation of hand-held models. As well as highly portable cameras of a conventional type, the last years of the nineteenth century saw a rash of novelties spring up: cameras were designed to look like postal packages or handbags, or made to be concealed in the hat or, with a lens peeping through a button-hole, in the waistcoat. In Russia the Tsar's secret police made use (or, at least, ordered a consignment) of cameras masquerading as pocket watches. But the craze for camouflaged cameras, never very serious, had largely died out by 1900, and surviving family cameras are more likely to date from the twentieth century and the Brownie revolution. Like photographs, cameras can, of course, be dated: fully bakelite bodies are not earlier than 1928; coloured cameras with decorated front panels are likely to belong to the late twenties or to the thirties, when, in an attempt to exploit the female market more fully, models were designed to fit in with a set of colour co-ordinated accessories such as compacts and lipstick holders. The identification and dating of cameras, however, is not the present concern, and one possible source of help for the interested reader is to be found in the bibliography.

A tremendous range of cameras was made, and there is a fair chance that something may have survived of the fair selection likely to have been used over the years in any one family. Box cameras and folding bellows cameras were both popular with amateurs, the choice depending largely on the user's pretentions to seriousness, and good numbers of both kinds may still be found. It may, too, be possible to buy very cheaply examples of what has not been inherited but is known to have been used. I now have a Kodak Brownie number 2, of the kind with which my father started to take pictures, and an Ensign Ful-Vue, of the kind with which I began. Though they are not the actual cameras we used, there is some satisfaction in having them to complement the 1930s folding Brownie 620 to which he, and later I, graduated.

If an ancestral camera has been preserved, one should not overlook the possibility that it still works. Box cameras, in particular, have very little to go wrong. In fact, finding appropriate film is far more likely to prove a problem than persuading the camera itself to function.

Stereoscopes

Like the family album, the stereoscope became a standard item of entertainment in many Victorian homes. Of the various kinds that were produced, the one which had widest use was that invented by the American writer, Oliver Wendell Holmes. Designed in 1860, Holmes' stereoscope continued in use, with small modifications over the years, well into the twentieth century. It was less awkward to handle than some earlier kinds, it was cheap to produce, and its success means that it is the most likely kind to be discovered amongst family memorabilia.

Holmes' stereoscope was a mask-like structure held before the eyes by a handle protruding below, rather like a cumbersome lorgnette. A flat runner stuck out in front of the mask, and on this was a cross-piece, which had supports to hold the card, and which could be slid backwards or forwards along the runner until the picture, viewed through the eyeholes of the mask, came into focus. More luxurious models were mounted on a stand rather than held by a handle.

If a stereoscope has been handed down without accompanying photographs, it is worth looking out for some at collectors' fairs. The pictures would not be of family significance but the stereoscope would be used again, and there is something satisfying about old objects continuing to serve their purpose. If buying stereo cards, it is worth making sure that they will fit one's viewer. Some people have a good eye for sizes; others carry a tape measure.

Frames

Fairly ornate frames started to appear early in the history of photography. Carved wooden frames with plaster mouldings were used as early as the 1840s to display daguerrotypes on a wall. Frames in all manner of designs and materials survive, of which the most attractive (and often the most valuable) are those in the art nouveau style. Even if it were possible to give quick pointers towards dating frames it would be of dubious assistance, since there is no reason to assume that a frame and its contents are contemporaneous. Photographs about the house today are not necessarily in frames of the same age, and we should not expect our forefathers to show any greater concern in the matter than we show ourselves.

Of the hinged case, used as a portable frame for daguerrotypes, ambrotypes or even tintypes with delusions of grandeur, something has already been said. It might be added that the same basic style, with pinchbeck surround and an outer frame of leather, papier-mâché or, perhaps, thermoplastic, was also frequently used for small open frames with no folding cover.

One further point that might be made about frames is that things are often other than they seem. Just as all that glisters is not gold, so all that bears a grain is not wood. Plaster, cardboard or papier-mâché could be painted or covered in paper with a wood or leather effect, and grain may derive from a brush rather than from growth rings.

Albums

Cartomania created a need for storage and display, and thus the family album was born. Albums were produced for cartes and, before long, for cabinet prints or a mixture of the two. They formed both a pictorial family archive and a source of entertainment and conversation.

Pages were made of thick card, for they had to accommodate two pictures slotted back-to-back into each cut-out space provided. The pages might be plain, but in the larger albums a fair proportion of them were decorated with illustrations. Flowers were very popular, as were waterside scenes, and snowscapes, swallows, swans, cornfields and romantic ruins all made their appearance. The better pictures were quite delicately done and have a distinct charm.

If the pages could be pretty, the bindings could be sumptuous. Leather was common, was generally padded, and could be heavily embossed or gilded. Some had mother-of-pearl set in and some incorporated a musical movement. Many were fastened with a metal clasp, and metal might also be used to protect the corners. The modern owner of a family album may well possess a very attractive volume, quite apart from the interest and appeal of its contents.

In an inherited album it is important to keep the photographs in their original positions. The owner will, of course, wish to slip the photographs out, study the backs and check the margins for any handwritten note obscured when the picture sits in the album. To avoid wear and tear on the picture surrounds, the researcher would be wise to make a note of information from the back before replacing the picture. It may be helpful to use a numbered sheet of notes for each page of the album, dividing the sheet according to the number and position of photographs on the page, and writing the notes in the space corresponding to the photograph. In this way writing on original pictures and album pages is avoided, and the removal of cartes and cabinets is kept to a minimum. To notes dealing with information on the reverse may be added any identification and dating that can be suggested, along with cross-reference to other examples thought to be showing the same sitter. Keeping photographs in their original positions matters, because those positions may be significant in identifying the subjects. A husband and wife may face each other; children may have been arranged in order of age; generation order may have been preserved, with the earliest pictures quite possibly predating the album itself.

Amongst the pleasures of looking through an album may be tracing family resemblances and finding images of the same person at different ages. It should be borne in mind, however, that it is easy to jump to false conclusions. The photographs may have been rearranged many times and may not all be of family: friends, neighbours and in-laws may all be included, too.

With the demise of cartes and cabinet prints and with the advent of roll film, there appeared photographs that were of various sizes and photographs that were not mounted on card. Plain pages, to which photographs could be attached, became more appropriate, and the age of the family album as a rich and hefty volume was over.

Negatives

Of glass negatives, the gelatin dry-plates would seem the more likely to be encountered today, since they are more recent, and since the earlier wet collodion plates were commonly stripped and recycled. Nevertheless, wet collodion plates have survived. Identification may not be easy, but the wet plates may prove to be more unevenly coated at the edges: the coating was an individual, on-the-spot process and often had to be hurried. There is even the chance of a thumb-sized, uncoated corner being found, where the plate, like the heel of the baby Achilles, was held during treatment. 1880 is a rough watershed date to mark the change from the wet to the dry negative process.

Roll film negatives have already been touched on, in dealing with pictures produced from them. Those from the early decades of the twentieth century have usually been cut up into individual images, and they can come in a wide variety of sizes, of which 2¼″ × 3¼″ was the most popular over the longest period. The earliest celluloid film, nitro-cellulose, was highly inflammable. It should be treated with respect, for auto-combustion is possible, and, in the early days of the cinema, such film was the cause of more than one disastrous fire. Safety film came into use in the early 1930s but did not completely replace nitro-cellulose film until about 1950. Knowing whether or not a negative is on safety film will not, therefore, provide a clear indication of date. A thin shaving cut from an old negative will readily produce a satisfying flare-up, whereas safety film is distinctly reluctant to catch fire, but for a period of about twenty years both kinds existed side by side.

One fairly short-lived development was the Autographic film. Some Kodak cameras had a small door in the back, which could be opened while details of date or subject were written with a metal stylus on the film's special backing paper. Where the backing paper was thus written on, it lost its opacity and the light passed through on to the actual film, with the inscription appearing as black lettering when the film was processed. Such inscriptions were made on the narrow strip between images. They thus appeared on the negatives but not on the positives that were made from them. A negative bearing writing revealed in the processing (rather than written on afterwards) dates from the period 1914, when suitable cameras were first produced, to 1933, when the specially backed film was discontinued.

Whatever kind of negative has been passed down, whether on glass or celluloid, the obvious thing to do is to make a print of it. Photographic chemicals and paper are not cheap, but simple contact prints can be made without the expense of an enlarger. The owner of an enlarger might, in fact, find the machine unable to cope with anything other than modern film sizes. Older negatives are, in any case, usually of dimensions sufficient to make a contact print worth having.

Copying Photographs

The Standard Method

The family historian may be the outright owner of a number of ancestral pictures, but others are often lent to be copied and returned. Sometimes, too, it is desirable to have duplicate pictures to pass on to relations, in appreciation of information given or to prompt further memories. Having pictures copied professionally can be expensive, and there is no reason why a little self-help should not be attempted, at least by those who already have a suitable camera. The amateur may start copying for the reasons already mentioned, but a bonus may soon be discovered: old, battered, creased photographs often look better in the copy than in the original. A brief outline of copying procedures may therefore be useful.

The first necessity is a single lens reflex (SLR) camera with through-the-lens metering. Readers who have such a camera will know that they do; others are not advised to go out and buy one just for the sake of making an occasional copy. Colour print film is used, since this reproduces the warm tone of old pictures which are rarely simply black and white. Relatively slow film, say 50 or 100 ASA, produces the sharpest image.

It is impossible to bring a standard camera close enough for a small object, such as a photograph, to fill the frame without the image becoming blurred and out of focus. This problem is overcome by adding close-up lenses or an extension tube or bellows to the camera. Each of these devices allows the photographer to move in very close to the subject without losing focus, and it can be possible to fill the frame with even a carte de visite. Of these additions, sets of close-up lenses are the cheapest. They are probably not the choice of the perfectionist, but photographers wishing to spend only a few pounds have no difficulty in persuading themselves that the results are quite satisfactory.

The next requirement is something to hold the camera steady – either a proper copy-stand or a very solid and stable tripod. This will hold the camera in position, pointing downwards at the original, which lies on a flat, horizontal surface. Attempting to fix the original to a vertical surface can cause it damage, and it is much harder to be sure that the camera is square on to a vertical subject. When the camera is pointing downwards, such problems can be solved with a spirit level. When positioning the camera, the photographer should remember to allow for the fact that, even though SLR cameras let us see what the lens sees, they take in a little more than can be seen through the viewfinder.

Flash is not a suitable form of illumination. Two photoflood lamps, each lighting from a side, can be positioned to avoid glare. If the original wants to curl in the heat of the lights, a sheet of glass can be used to hold it flat. This, of course, can give considerable opportunities for reflections, but adjustment of the photofloods should resolve any difficulty. Since artificial lighting creates a warm colour cast on normal daylight film, the camera will have to be fitted with a daylight-to-artificial-light conversion filter.

With original and camera both in position and with lighting set up, it just remains to take the picture. Set the exposure according to the meter reading, taking two pictures on slightly different settings if in doubt. The use of a cable-release mechanism bypasses any chance of the hand causing the camera to shake.

The film, when exposed, can be processed in the usual way at the local shop of your choice. If more than one copy of a picture is wanted, it is worth bearing in mind that a series of identical shots on the same film usually costs less than a series of prints made from the same shot.

Cheating

The method so far described is the standard one adopted by serious photographers. There is, however, a simplified method which can be used by those who are only half serious. The SLR camera and a close-up attachment are still needed, but copy-stand, photofloods, conversion filter and cable-release can all be dispensed with. Whether or not the method is satisfactory is very much up to the individual. Readers with meticulously high standards in such matters should probably move straight on to the next section.

The camera is hand-held and natural light is used. There is no need to set up shop out of doors; a well-lit indoor site, such as a desk or table at a window, is suitable. Even bright, direct sunlight is not necessary; good indoor daylight will do. Of course, it is necessary to use a film that reacts more quickly to the light. 400 ASA films are readily obtainable and serve very well. It is true that faster film speeds tend to produce grainier results, but in practice an effect which might be a nuisance with a slide, much magnified in projection, may be negligible on a postcard-sized print.

Since the original is placed on the desk or table top, the photographer has to lean over, pointing the camera downwards. Whilst it is important to avoid a shadow being cast over the original, the fact that the light is coming from the other side of the desk means that few problems are likely to be experienced. With the close-up lenses (or more expensive equivalent) in place, and with the focus set down to its shortest distance, one moves oneself and the camera up and down until the picture is clear. It may turn out that not enough of the subject is in the frame, in which case readjustment of both focus and photographer will be needed. When it comes to the final, fine adjustments, though, it is easier to move oneself than to alter the focus. Then, with exposure set according to metering, take the picture. Having released the shutter, relax, then go through the process again to take a second shot. Human error, such as unsteadiness of hand or failure to hold the camera absolutely square to the subject, is very possible with this method, which is why it is a good idea to make assurance doubly sure. A few extra pictures cost far less than the equipment needed for the serious-minded method.

The use of natural light obviates any need for conversion filters. But it is even possible to make constructive use of the effects of artificial light. When copying some modern black and white copies of unavailable originals, I tried the experiment of adding the light of a standard lamp to the sunlight coming through the window. The colour cast created by this diluted electric light gave a not disagreeable sepia effect to the end results, restoring something of the antique flavour that the unseen originals would have had.

This cheating method is open to criticism. It is nevertheless likely to improve on the original, since modern copies often have a cosmetic way with imperfections and restore lost contrast. The worn edges of an original can be cut out by bringing the camera a little closer, and the end product can be surprisingly pleasing. The pure- and high-minded are not to be scorned for not being satisfied with such an arbitrary procedure; but lesser mortals, willing to have a go, may be very happy with the results.

Looking after Old Photographs

Photographs are not for ever. Fugitive images on fragile or flimsy material, they are patently vulnerable. Nevertheless, many have lasted far longer than the people they depict, thanks in part to their sentimental value and an unwillingness to throw them away when all about them is consigned to the bonfire or the tip. But our early pictures, which have so far survived the process of growing old, the wear and tear of being handled, the rough and tumble of storage in a shoe box or the back of a drawer, are still at great risk: excessive heat and dryness can embrittle and crack them; moisture, especially in warm conditions, can promote fungal growth; chemicals, contained both in the pictures themselves and in the materials they are stored in, can interact, stain and cause fading.

Faced with a threat to valuable possessions, the owner can do two things: look after them safely, and take out insurance. In the case of photographs, insurance amounts to making copies. Where, as with family portraits, the image is of at least as much value as the artefact, it makes sense to provide oneself with duplicates. As for the looking after, the steps to be taken are up to the individual. Effective conservation of a collection of photographs can be a costly business, and the notes which follow may in places go beyond what a non-specialist collector feels able to do. But they also cover common-sense measures that may be taken without undue expense.

Handling and Using

In art galleries we go along readily enough with instructions not to touch the exhibits. What is good for the Mona Lisa is good enough for great-great-grandma. Even clean skin exudes chemicals. So photographs should be handled only at the extreme edges, adding support from the back if necessary; touching the actual image should be avoided.

Once photographs have been identified, they need to be labelled in some way. Adhesive labels are to be shunned, for they peel off in time, leaving a stain. Ink markings on the back could eventually bleed through to the face of the photograph, and hard writing implements engrave their message, so that a few words on the reverse are liable to give an unwanted relief impression on the image itself. A soft lead pencil is not only gentler in its action, but it can even, if required, be erased, thus enabling one to abide by the dictum that nothing should ever be done to a photograph that cannot be reversed. The amount of writing on the back can be reduced by the use of reference codes, linked to detailed notes recorded separately. Where photographs are kept in an old family album it is possible, as previously indicated, to keep records without marking them at all.

Light

The light that made photographs can also destroy them. Fading caused by chemicals used in the original process may not be avoidable, but bleaching in the sunlight is. Artificial light is no great friend to photographs either, but fluorescent light is particularly hostile, being rather similar to the sun in its effect.

It follows that photographs should be stored in the dark. Often, however, there is a wish to display some of them. Such pictures should be placed where they do not bask in natural light as it moves around the room. The window wall itself is usually protected, unless there are windows in more than one wall, and other walls may prove to be well shaded. When the direction of light is considered, it should be borne in mind that this varies not just with time of day but also with time of year: the low winter sun may seek out spots that remain relatively shaded in summer.

There is, of course, a simple solution to the problem of display, and that is to put only copies on view, keeping the originals tucked away in the gloom.

Temperature and Humidity

A relatively dry environment should be sought in which to keep photographs. Too dry an area can, admittedly, cause its own problems, such as encouraging silverfish, which like nothing better than a good meal of gelatine. But the fact remains that humidity is the most alarming cause of deterioration in photographs.

Relative coolness is also desirable, as heat can damage and can add to the dangers of both excessive dryness and excessive humidity. Particularly to be avoided is a place with varying extremes of temperature, for a photograph is made up of a number of layers, each of which expands and contracts at its own rate as it warms and cools.

It may not be possible to control the home as if it were a professional archive, but dryness and reasonable constancy of moderate temperature can be aimed at. With such considerations in mind, certain domestic storage sites are clearly unsuitable. Living rooms are likely to become very warm, for human tastes differ from those of photographs. Such rooms may have a live fire, and coal gives off by-products that are potentially harmful. Kitchens and bathrooms are steamy, attics are dusty, garages are for pollutant-emitting cars, and conservatories are temperature's equivalent of the yo-yo. When unthinkable places have been ruled out, what is left is likely to be a bedroom or, perhaps, a study, and even there proximity to a heating source is undesirable.

Storage

Once a room has been chosen, storage containers and materials have to be selected, for the photographs need to be protected from dust. Dust, after all, is only free-range sandpaper. But storage presents its own problem, for chemically inert materials do not grow on trees.

Wood does grow on trees, and it contains lignin, a cell-stiffening substance inimical to photographs. Cabinets and boxes of new or untreated wood are therefore not recommended. Old, seasoned wood, however, is likely to have passed its avoid-by date. Metal shelves and cabinets are generally considered safe, as long as they are enamelled rather than painted.

Inside a cabinet, sleeves, envelopes or wrappings are likely to be needed. Paper and cardboard are the obvious materials, but if made, as they almost certainly will be, from wood pulp, they too contain lignin. Plastic is also highly suspect. Pure polyester and polypropylene are currently considered acceptable, but many other kinds are warned against. PVC is rated Public Enemy Number One, for the chemicals employed in its manufacture can migrate to those surfaces that it touches. It is possible to obtain safe plastic sleeves and paper made from cotton or purified wood fibre, and further details may be found in the books mentioned in the bibliography. It should be added, to increase the reader's sense of depression at this point, that views on what is safe could well change, since the problems relating to any one storage material, especially one that is new, may become apparent only with the passing of time.

Photograph albums are a further problem, and the ideal album has probably yet to be produced. Certainly those modern albums which use self-seal transparent pages should not be countenanced. Their adhesive coating can discolour with remarkable speed, and many photographers will no more use them for their new pictures than for their treasured heirlooms. Old albums are probably by now relatively safe, and they should be retained. The ordering of photographs within them may in itself be informative, and their window mounts offer good protection, Indeed, window mounts are an effective device for retaining pictures. In their absence, hinges may be made, using a genuinely water-soluble adhesive and not, it need hardly be said, sticky tape. Corner mounts may also be considered. What they are made of may be open to question, but at least they come into contact with only a very small area of the image.

Photographs and celluloid negatives should normally be stored horizontally. If they are kept upright, they should be packed firmly enough to ensure against curling or slipping. Glass negatives in any number should not be stored flat, because of the considerable weight that those at the bottom of a pile would have to bear.

The combustible properties of cellulose nitrate negatives have already been mentioned. In practice, self-ignition is only likely in very warm conditions, and when the negatives are already in an advanced state of decomposition. Accidents have generally been associated with cellulose nitrate cine film, which was tightly rolled in well-sealed containers. It would seem sensible, therefore, to store any such negatives separately in a cool, dry place, neither tightly nor airtightly packed, and to check their condition periodically.

Prevention and Cure

The owner of old photographs must decide what kind of protection it is reasonable to attempt. Compromises may have to be made, and I am careful to avoid claims to practising all that I preach. It is, however, evident that some thought and care are worthwhile.

If first-aid measures are required, to repair or retouch, expert advice should be sought. Retouching can be attempted on a copy, but unschooled ministrations to creased, torn or damaged originals are not recommended. Heroic conservation, like heroic surgery, is the province of the professional.

Photographs and Dating Charts

For ease of use the photographs are arranged on pages 62 – 79. The charts which follow them serve for quick reference. Where details are briefly or cryptically described, a fuller explanation may also be found in the text.

It should be borne in mind that dates on the charts can often be only approximate. In particular, practices may have survived with individual photographers, and clothes in individual families, rather later than can be indicated by any general statement about dates.

A modest but nicely finished ambrotype. The buttons and jewellery have been touched with gilt.

A good, precise ambrotype image: knuckles, bow and sidewhiskers are all reproduced in fine detail. A small crescent of the backing varnish has flaked away below the left hand.

*The image of this tintype is
brighter than many but the
emulsion has bubbled and the
oval shape in the pinchbeck
has been cut roughly by hand.*

*Gem tintype from Taylor's
American Gem Studio,
Bradford. The tintype is
held in place by a patch
of paper stuck on the
back.*

A carte de visite from the 1860s, as crinoline, squared corners, simple classical setting and simple trade plate on the back all indicate.

Carte de visite from the 1890s, showing the period's love of lace on blouses. The vignetted head-and-shoulders portrait is typical of the time.

The reverse of this carte shows the kind of publicity material that the mounts carried. Medals, royal arms and Prince of Wales' feathers are all featured.

A cherub photographer with butterfly wings appears on the reverse of this elaborate 1890s carte mount.

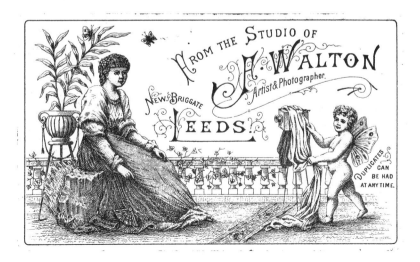

*Cabinet print on a gold-
lettered, dark mount, which
suggests the 1890s. The
leg-of-mutton sleeves belong
to the middle of the decade.*

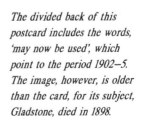

*The divided back of this
postcard includes the words,
'may now be used', which
point to the period 1902–5.
The image, however, is older
than the card, for its subject,
Gladstone, died in 1898.*

*Stereo card: Castle Rising
Castle. No ancestral link,
but now the author's
neighbourhood Norman castle.*

*One of a set of pictures
of the Norwich floods of
1912. Printed from a
roll-film negative.*

Squared corners and classical studio setting, with chair as ornament rather than seat, suggest the late 1860s for this carte of 'Sophie's little sister'.

The chair for leaning on and the window giving on to a rural scene point to the 70s or late 60s. Squared corners & trade-plate back belong more to the earlier part of this period.

J.A.SYKES.   LINDLEY.

Annie Kay, aged 18, sits
in front of choppy canvas
waves with a romantic pile
in the background. The carte
is dated 18th March 1888.

Tintype with bubbled surface,
presented as a birthday card.
It was not unusual to mark a
birthday or Christmas with a
small photograph.

*The simplicity of setting
and hairstyles, the sloping
shoulders and full skirts,
and the fact that the oldest
girl's ears are hidden
combine to suggest the first
half of the 1860s for this
carte. Note that skirt
lengths relate to age.*

*Carte: Harriet & Robert
Hewsole, Lucknow, December
1864. Tartan was popular
for children at the time.
Robert still wears a skirt.*

*Squared corners, simple setting
& full-length seated figure all
indicate the 1860s. Since ears
were commonly exposed in the
mid 60s and crinolines were
less popular as the 70s
approached, about 1865 seems
a fair guess.*

BARRATT.   TORQUAY.

*The full-length seated figure
in a simple setting is
characteristic of cartes of
the 60s. Note the raised
trouser-seams. The curved
line of the hat's brim
points to the second half
of the decade.*

Carte: jabots, heavily trimmed dresses, hair & skirts bunched back, sleeves set in at the shoulder, padded lectern & over-all design on the reverse all speak of the 1870s.

The picture is mounted on a thin, uninformative piece of card, but the fussinesss of neck and cuffs, as well as the architecture of the hair, point to the 1870s.

Outdoor set with fence and gate, sloping bustle, fringing and mixture of materials indicate the 1870s, and the epaulette effect went out early in the decade. The carte is dated September 1871.

The hair (some of it her own), scarf-bow and padded chair all suggest the 1870s. That the photographer was Mrs Robinson of Ashton-under-Lyne serves to remind us that men had no monopoly over photography.

*Front & back of the same
cabinet print. The Little
Lord Fauntleroy look is
associated with the 1880s,
but the dark, ornate card
mount suggests the 1890s.
A late example of fashion
and an early example of
mount would seem likely.
The reverse, printed in
gold on dark green,
includes cherub, pheasant,
shield, flowers, camera.*

1875 is printed on the back of this French carte, but the uncompromising projection of the bustle suggests its reincarnation in the early 1880s.

The carte's dark, gold-lettered mount may suggest the 1890s, but it must date from a few years earlier, since Maria Bush left England for Hawaii in 1888.

Copy of a cabinet print: Edith Pols, with her first four children, 1893/4. If the children's ages didn't date the picture, her sleeves would. The sailor look was still popular and the taste for tartan was not wholly dead.

Cabinet print showing the vignette effect favoured in the 1890s. Comparison of the photographer's address with Norwich directories puts the date at about 1892.

Shrubsole

EXCHANGE S.ᵗ
& DAVEY PLACE
NORWICH

ELECTRIC &
DAYLIGHT
STUDIO.

Frederick J. Boyes

DERBY.

Cabinet print: the sitter looks surprisingly young to be still wearing a taped indoor cap in (as the reverse reveals) the middle or late 1890s.

A carte de visite showing the leg-of-mutton sleeves that were in vogue in the mid-1890s.

Hellis & Sons   PHOTOGRAPHERS

Enlarged section of a
roll-film photograph.
The huge hat points
firmly to the years
just before the
First World War.

The young Arthur Bush,
c1912. The USA Studios
(in Croydon) were still
producing carte-sized
photos, though they were
not card-backed. Note
the supporting hands.

J. L. CARTER,   UNION MILLS, PA.

Carte showing the problems of establishing the sitter's age. The carte is American, and the subject, Sarah Comer's sister, is aged 54. Compare her with today's well-preserved and pampered half-centenarians.

Postcard: the Scoffin family at the seaside. Really too late for this book, but the photographer's kindness in providing a date, and the juxtaposition of jolly logo and grim weather, combine to make it hard to resist.

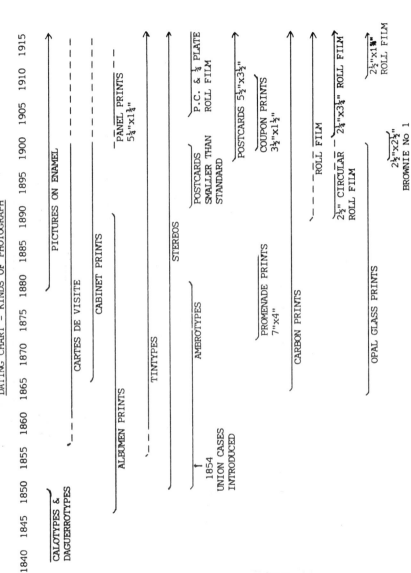

DATING CHART – KINDS OF PHOTOGRAPH

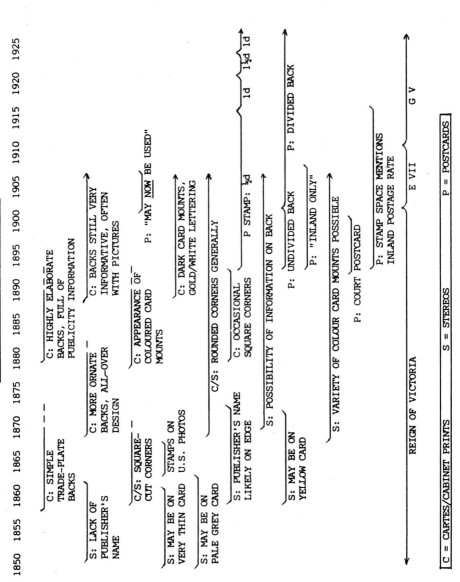

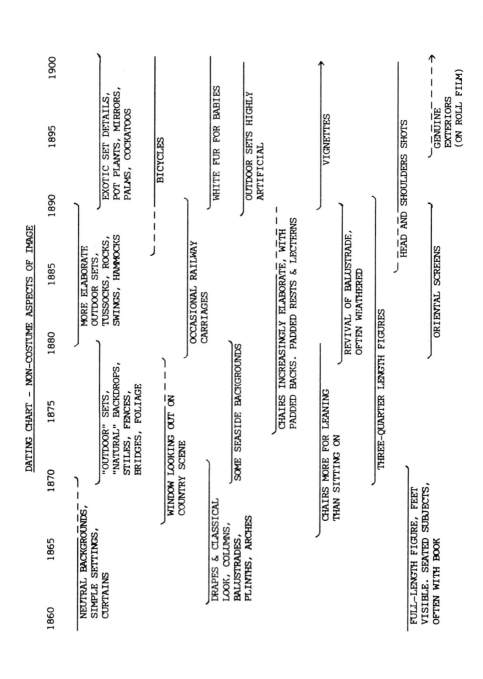

DATING CHART – NON-COSTUME ASPECTS OF IMAGE

1860   1865   1870   1875   1880   1885   1890   1895   1900

NEUTRAL BACKGROUNDS, SIMPLE SETTINGS, CURTAINS

"OUTDOOR" SETS, "NATURAL" BACKDROPS, STILES, FENCES, BRIDGES, FOLIAGE

MORE ELABORATE OUTDOOR SETS, TUSSOCKS, ROCKS, SWINGS, HAMMOCKS

EXOTIC SET DETAILS, POT PLANTS, MIRRORS, PALMS, COCKATOOS

WINDOW LOOKING OUT ON COUNTRY SCENE

BICYCLES

DRAPES & CLASSICAL LOOK, COLUMNS, BALUSTRADES, PLINTHS, ARCHES

OCCASIONAL RAILWAY CARRIAGES

WHITE FUR FOR BABIES

SOME SEASIDE BACKGROUNDS

OUTDOOR SETS HIGHLY ARTIFICIAL

CHAIRS INCREASINGLY ELABORATE, WITH PADDED BACKS. PADDED RESTS & LECTERNS

CHAIRS MORE FOR LEANING THAN SITTING ON

REVIVAL OF BALUSTRADE, OFTEN WEATHERED

VIGNETTES

THREE-QUARTER LENGTH FIGURES

HEAD AND SHOULDERS SHOTS

FULL-LENGTH FIGURE, FEET VISIBLE. SEATED SUBJECTS, OFTEN WITH BOOK

ORIENTAL SCREENS

GENUINE EXTERIORS (ON ROLL FILM)

DATING CHART – WOMEN'S CLOTHES: GENERAL LINE AND DECORATION

1840 1845 1850 1855 1860 1865 1870 1875 1880 1885 1890 1895 1900 1905 1910 1915

SLEEVES FAIRLY
CLOSE-FITTING:
SKIRT SMOOTH &
BELL-SHAPED

GEOMETRICAL
PATTERNS

TIGHT CORSETRY

1871 – INTRODUCTION OF
DOLLY VARDEN DRESS

TAILORED SUIT
WITH BLOUSE

TUBULAR
DRESS,
HOBBLE SKIRT

SLEEK, NARROWER
CUT TO SKIRT &
SLEEVES

BODICE ABOVE CRINOLINE
CUT TO MOULD FIGURE

HIGH BUSTLE, STICKING
OUT HORIZONTALLY

JET & LACE

BLOUSE & SKIRT
COMBINATION POPULAR

CRINOLINES

PRINCESS LINE, WAIST TIGHT,
LONG, COMING TO A POINT

SKIRTS PLAIN; FASHION
EMPHASIS ON TOP HALF
OF BODY

SLOPING LINE
TO BUSTLE

LEG-OF-MUTTON
SLEEVES

COMPLICATED DESIGNS;
MIXTURE OF COLOURS &
MATERIALS IN SAME DRESS

BASIC DRESS DESIGN BECOMING
PLAINER, BUT PLENTY OF
DECORATION STILL ADDED

S-SHAPED, HEAVY BUSTED
LOOK (LESS PRONOUNCED
FROM c1908)

INCREASED USE OF LACE;
FEATHER BOAS

LOTS OF TRIMMINGS:
FRILLS, RIBBONS,
STITCHING, BUTTONS,
FRINGING

'NATURAL HISTORY'
DECORATION ON
DRESSES & HATS

'NATURAL HISTORY' DECORATION
MORE SUBDUED; MAINLY ON HATS

DATING CHART – WOMEN'S CLOTHES: BODICE, SLEEVES, SKIRT

1840 1845 1850 1855 1860 1865 1870 1875 1880 1885 1890 1895 1900 1905 1910 1915

BODICE CUT TO MOULD FIGURE

SQUARE YOKE, BRAIDED OR FRINGED

FIGURE-FITTING BODICE BUTTONED TO THROAT

ELABORATE BLOUSES, BOLEROS,

BLOUSES & BOLEROS VERY POPULAR & VERY ELABORATE

SLEEVE FITTED FAIRLY CLOSE TO ARM

SIMPLE BODICES, HIGH-SET SLEEVES

JACKETS & JACKET-STYLE DRESS BODICES

MORE SOFTLY DRAPED SKIRTS

SLOPING SHOULDER; WIDE, LONG SLEEVES

NARROW SLEEVES PEAKED AT SHOULDER

CLOSE-FITTING SLEEVES & PUFFED SHOULDER

UPPER SLEEVE PUFFED, LOW-SET

CUIRASSE BODICE

LEG-OF-MUTTON SLEEVE

TIGHT WAIST, BELL-SHAPED SKIRTS, EMPHASIS ON CURVES, OFTEN WITH TRAIN

EPAULETTES, OFTEN BRAIDED

EPAULETTES DISAPPEAR

¾ SLEEVE, FRILLED

SLEEVES HIGHER, SET IN AT SHOULDER

SIMPLER SKIRTS, SMOOTH OVER HIPS, FLARED, GORED

HOBBLE SKIRTS

SMOOTH, BELL-SHAPED SKIRTS

CAGE CRINOLINE

BUSTLE GOES; SKIRTS FULL AT BACK

FLOPPY WAISTED BLOUSE DISAPPEARS

SKIRTS LESS FULL

SLOPING BUSTLE

HIGHER BUSTLE

SKIRTS INCREASINGLY FULL

FLAT-FRONTED SKIRTS

OVERSKIRTS DISAPPEAR

LONG SLEEVES, TIGHT AT WRIST; MAYBE FULLER AT TOP; COVERING PART OF HAND

DATING CHART – WOMEN'S FASHIONS: HEAD AND NECK

1840 1845 1850 1855 1860 1865 1870 1875 1880 1885 1890 1895 1900 1905 1910 1915

HAIR IN DANGLING SIDE RINGLETS, BUN AT BACK

CENTRAL PARTING, EARS COVERED

BY 1855, INDOOR CAPS LARGELY DISCARDED BY SINGLE YOUNGER WOMEN

PRINCESS ALEXANDRA STYLE FRINGE

SOME FRINGES, OFTEN CRIMPED, TOUSLED, STRAGGLY

HAIR HIGH ON HEAD

ORNATE HAIRSTYLES, ARTIFICIAL HAIR; BACK OF HEAD ECHOES SHAPE OF BACK OF SKIRT

HATS TRIMMED WITH WILDLIFE

HAIR OFTEN IN BUN; FRINGES RARE

PLAIN HAIRSTYLES, SMOOTHED BACK INTO BUN FROM CENTRAL PARTING

EARS EXPOSED

SIMPLER HAIR FOLLOWING LINE OF HEAD

ENORMOUS HATS

CHIGNON HAIRSTYLE

BUN HIGH ON HEAD

BUN, IF WORN, AT BACK OF HEAD

BONNET WITH TIES & FORWARD-POINTING BRIM

PORK-PIE HAT SQUARE ON HEAD

BOATERS FOR WOMEN AS WELL AS MEN

HIGH NECKLINES, SMALL COLLARS & BROOCHES

INDOOR CAPS ONLY FOR OLDER, MARRIED WOMEN

VARIED NECKLINES, SCARVES, JABOTS

1896: INTRODUCTION OF DOOR-KNOCKER OR TEAPOT-HANDLE HAIRSTYLE: LOOP OR COIL AT BACK OF HEAD

STANDING COLLARS, BUTTONED TO THROAT, PIECRUST FRILLS

SMALL, WHITE INDOOR CAPS

HATS OFTEN SMALL, FIRMLY CENTRED

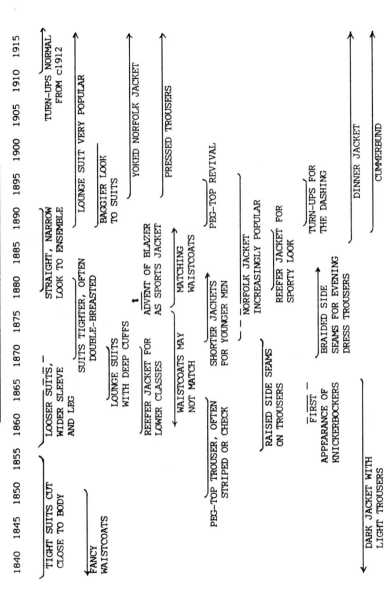

DATING CHART – MEN'S CLOTHES: TRUNK AND LIMBS

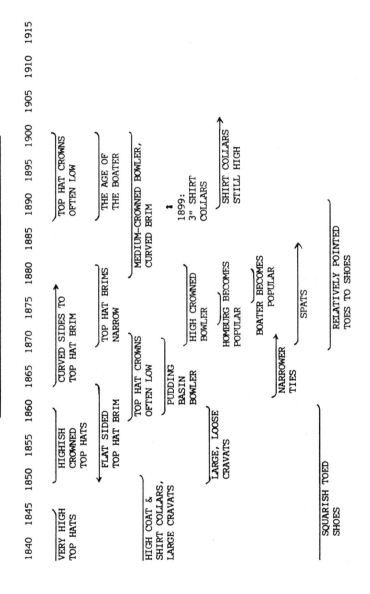

DATING CHART - MEN'S CLOTHES: HEAD, NECK AND FEET

1840 1845 1850 1855 1860 1865 1870 1875 1880 1885 1890 1895 1900 1905 1910 1915

VERY HIGH
TOP HATS

HIGHISH
CROWNED
TOP HATS

FLAT SIDED
TOP HAT BRIM

CURVED SIDES TO
TOP HAT BRIM

TOP HAT BRIMS
NARROW

TOP HAT CROWNS
OFTEN LOW

THE AGE OF
THE BOATER

HIGH COAT &
SHIRT COLLARS,
LARGE CRAVATS

TOP HAT CROWNS
OFTEN LOW

MEDIUM-CROWNED BOWLER,
CURVED BRIM

PUDDING
BASIN
BOWLER

HIGH CROWNED
BOWLER

1899:
3" SHIRT
COLLARS

SHIRT COLLARS
STILL HIGH

LARGE, LOOSE
CRAVATS

HOMBURG BECOMES
POPULAR

BOATER BECOMES
POPULAR

NARROWER
TIES

SPATS

SQUARISH TOED
SHOES

RELATIVELY POINTED
TOES TO SHOES

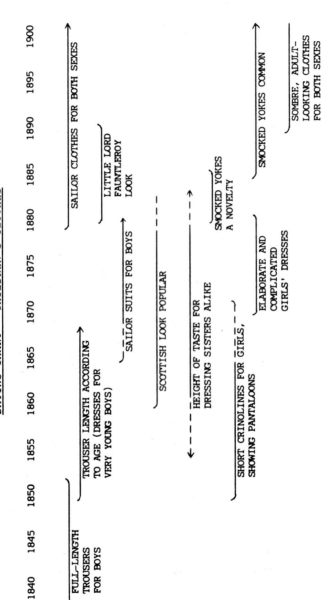

DATING CHART – CHILDREN'S CLOTHES

Bibliography

Since this bibliography is selective, personal and annotated, it runs the risk of being idiosyncratic. Whilst covering books dealing generally with early photography, it also places some emphasis on those which help with dating and those which pay some attention to the commercial and amateur photographers, whose work is most likely to be encountered by the family historian.

Early Photography

'The First Negatives', D.B.Thomas, HMSO, 1964.
Deals with calotypes especially, but also informative on the daguerrotype and wet collodion processes.

'Early Photography', Patrick Daniels, Academy Editions, 1978.
A fairly short general survey of photography up to the turn of the century.

'The Art of Photogenic Drawing', M.Seaborne, and 'The Calotype Process', R.E.Lassam, R.Morris and M.Seaborne, Fox Talbot Museum Information Leaflets, Numbers 1 & 2, undated.
These leaflets describe Fox Talbot's work, with directions for the authentic reproduction of his processes.

' "From today painting is dead" – The Beginnings of Photography', Arts Council of Great Britain, 1972.
Though this is, in fact, a catalogue to a V&A exhibition, it includes an essay on portrait photography by Tristram Powell, as well as useful notes on the early processes.

'Photography – A Concise History', Ian Jeffrey, Thames & Hudson, 1981.
Deals with the full history of photography but devotes more than 100 pages to the period before the First World War. More concerned with photographers than processes, and especially with photographers as artists.

'The Camera and its Images', Arthur Goldsmith, Ridge Press, 1979.
Another full history, though with a more broadly based approach, with over half the space devoted to the early period, and with some attention to the roll film revolution. Very readable and particularly well illustrated.

Help with Identification and Dating

'Victorian and Edwardian Photographs', Margaret F.Harker, Charles Letts, 1975.
   Intended as a general introduction, but with plenty of incidental help towards identifying and dating formats and processes.

'Family History in Focus', Don Steel & Lawrence Taylor, Lutterworth Press, 1984.
   Invaluable for identification and dating, and for wider consideration of photographs and the family historian. Also includes a chapter touching on the dating of military uniforms. Required reading.

'The Carte de Visite', David Cory, in 'Bygones 5', ed. Dick Joice, Boydell Press, 1980.
   Has some incidental comments on dating and a list of Norwich photographers as they appear in directories.

'Fashion à la Carte: 1861–1900', Avril Lansdell, Shire, 1985.
   Slim, cheap, and packed with information on dating by costume. Highly recommended.

'Victorian Dress in Photographs', Madeleine Ginsburg, Batsford, 1982.
   Full of helpfully annotated examples. Also highly recommended.

Popular Photography – Commercial and Amateur

'The Victorian Professional Photographer', John Hannavy, Shire, 1980.
   Deals with what the title claims, and with rather more than its contents page suggests.

'National Portrait Gallery – People in Camera 1839–1914', Colin Ford & Allan Porter, C.J.Bucher & Camera, 1979.
   Published for a National Portrait Gallery exhibition, and in conjunction with the Granada television series, 'Camera'. Concerned with portrait photography, with some attention to the work of the commercial photographer.

'The Story of Popular Photography', ed. Colin Ford, Century in association with the National Museum of Photography, Film & Television, 1989.
   Has a strong, and justified, Kodak orientation, and includes chapters on the mass market and the roll film revolution.

'Understanding Old Photographs', Robert Pols, Robert Boyd Publications, 1995.
   Looks at the making of early photographic images and at the messages they convey.

Conservation of Photographs

'Collecting and Preserving Old Photographs', Elizabeth Martin, Collins, 1988.
   Also includes chapters on history and identification, and explains the ways in which different kinds of photograph deteriorate.

'Caring for your Family Photographs at Home', Audrey Linkman, publisher not stated, 1991.
Accurately titled, inexpensive and authoritative.

Special Interests

'Optical Toys', Basil Harley, Shire, 1988.
Includes a short, illustrated account of the camera obscura.

'Collecting Picture Postcards – An Introduction', Anthony Byatt, Golden Age Postcard Books, 1982.
Aimed primarily at would-be collectors, but including some useful dating information.

'Discovering Old Cameras', Robert White, Shire, 1981.
Contains much incidental information to help with identification and dating of film formats as well as cameras.

Collected Examples of Early Photography

There is a long series, published by Batsford, of places and special interests, with titles following the pattern of 'Victorian and Edwardian Cambridge (or Northumbria, or Wales, or Railways, or Children) From Old Photographs'. Hendon Publishing has produced a series concentrating on early pictures of towns and cities, often under such a title as 'Harrogate (or Grimsby, or Coventry) As It Was'. Not all such books, however, come as part of a series. Many areas have inspired their own one-off collections of early photographs, and a look through the local interest section of a good bookshop should produce examples.

A selection of more general collections follows. Any such selection must be somewhat random, and other examples are easy to find. Shops dealing in publishers' remainders can be a very rewarding hunting ground.

'Edwardian Album', Nicolas Bentley, Cardinal, 1974.

'Victorian Life in Photographs', William Sansom, Thames & Hudson, 1974.

'Reality Recorded Early Documentary Photography', Gail Buckland, David and Charles, 1974.

'A Cockney Camera', Gordon Winter, Penguin, 1975.

'A Country Camera', Gordon Winter, Penguin, 1973.